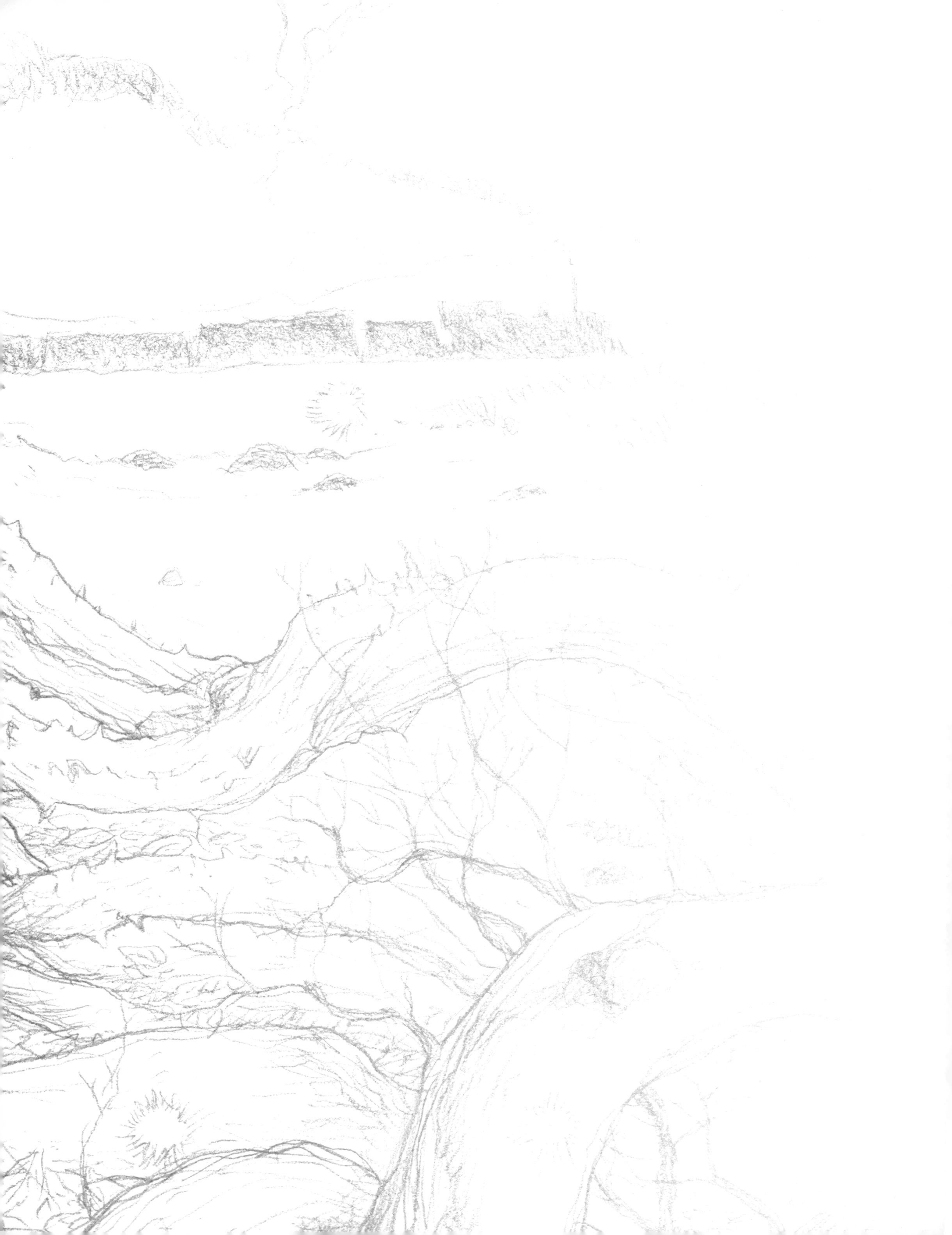

# A Glance Backward

Pierre Paquet                    Tony Sandoval

MAGNETIC PRESS
www.MAGNETIC-PRESS.com

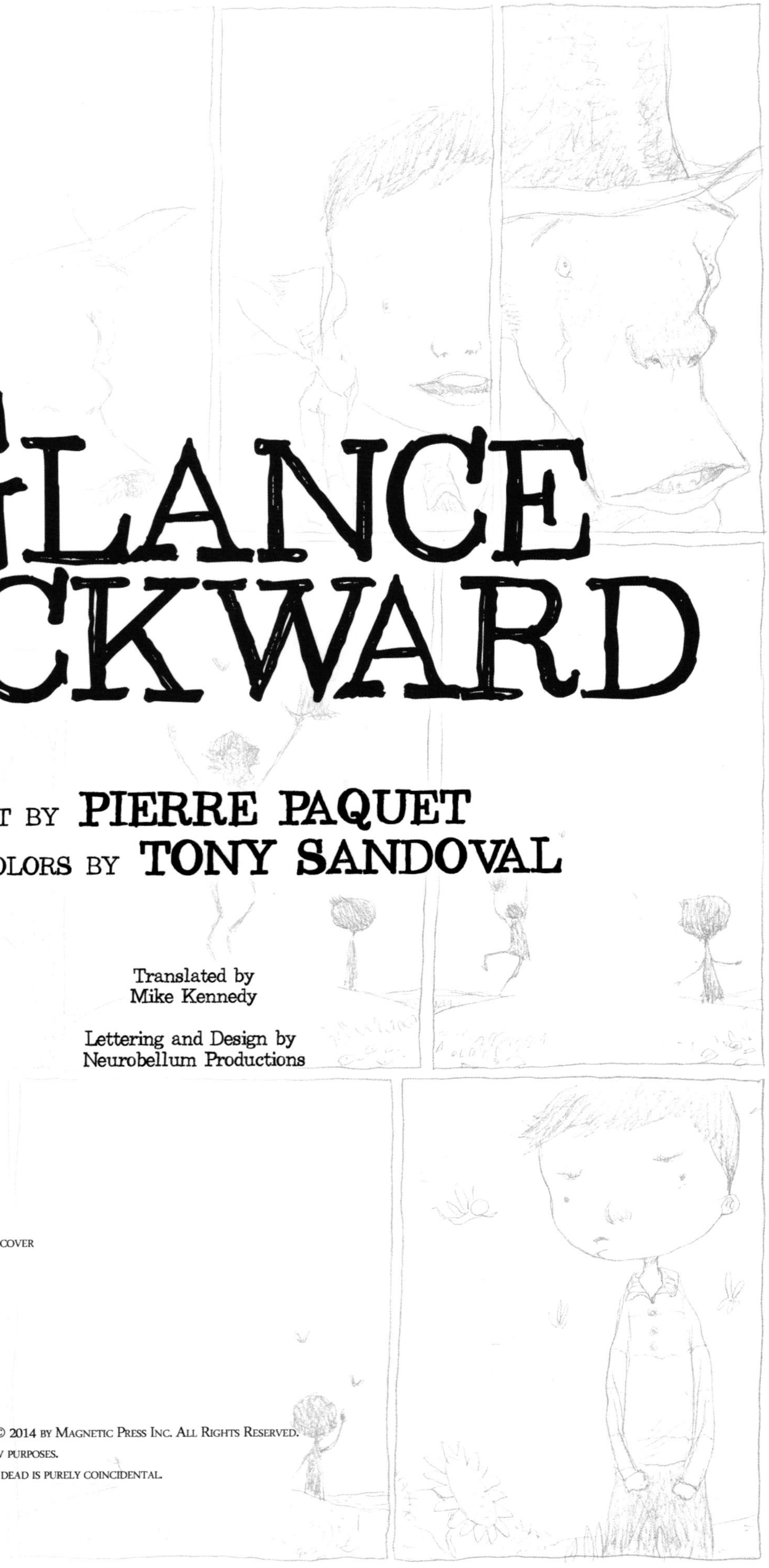

# A Glance Backward

Script by PIERRE PAQUET
Art and Colors by TONY SANDOVAL

Translated by
Mike Kennedy

Lettering and Design by
Neurobellum Productions

**MAGNETIC PRESS**
Mike Kennedy, *Publisher/President*
Wes Harris, *Vice President*
4910 N. Winthrop Ave #3
Chicago, IL 60640
**WWW.MAGNETIC-PRESS.COM**

**A GLANCE BACKWARD** Original Graphic Novel Hardcover
April 2015. FIRST PRINTING

ISBN: 978-1-942367-11-6

First published as *UN REGARD PAR DESSUS L'EPAULE*


Printed in China by Global PSD.

# FOREWORD

A few years ago I was on a quest. It's a familiar quest to those of us who love to find new and interesting comics and art styles. It usually involves us hunting through many websites and backpacking through a convention somewhere in the world and searching. Hunting. Looking for those books you've never heard of but will change the way you think about art and storytelling. There have been many quests over many years, but this quest brought me to the stack of books by Tony Sandoval.

I had followed Tony's work online for years and was a fan of his interpretation of the world. His lines were immediate and full of life. Each mark had a heart beat and would crawl around the page giving me so many new things to discover. I loved his work but it was difficult to find his books in the states, or to really know what books were out there. That's why I loved my quests and finally I had found the treasure.

I got his sketchbooks, a few other comics and a big, large format hardcover titled UN REGARD PAR DESSUS L'EPAULE. I had NO IDEA what that said but it had those lines on the cover. These living, breathing lines and they were moving and racing and building images of a boy with vines and roots plunging through his body. It was beautiful. It was haunting. But most of all, it was MINE! I paid quickly as if someone might not let me if I didn't. I put it in my backpack and breathed a sigh of relief that another quest had been completed.

Over the next few years I flipped through the pages of this book, soaking in a story I couldn't read with words but would feel through Tony's art. It was a boy on a journey... a quest. Like me. Looking for the answers? Looking for relief? Looking for peace? I didn't know, but I wanted to. I even found an app that would translate words in real time for the sole purpose of trying to read this book. The app didn't work; it felt like trying to read the book with the animated opening titles to Se7en. Nonetheless, this book became one of my favorites and I would reserve time each week for quick flip through.

Then one day I get an email from my buddy, Mike Kennedy. He asked me if I wouldn't mind reading a new book they'll be releasing called A GLANCE BACKWARD. He knows me and thinks I'll dig it. He had no idea of my previous quest and the treasure I found. He has no idea how excited I am to finally be able to read this book that has been living with me for so many days yet went unread. Books are meant to be read.

And then... I read this. The story was....

Well, I had to work VERY hard and wait a very long time to finally read this touching, beautiful coming of age story, so I'm not going to make it that easy for you. I'll tell you that if you were on a quest and this book is what you found at the end, it is a treasure indeed. Books are meant to be read... so go. Read.

Skottie Young, 2015
*Eisner Award winner, THE WONDERFUL WIZARD OF OZ*

DEDICATION

FOR MY SONS, GASPARD, BAUDOUIN & LÉOPOLD.

– PIERRE

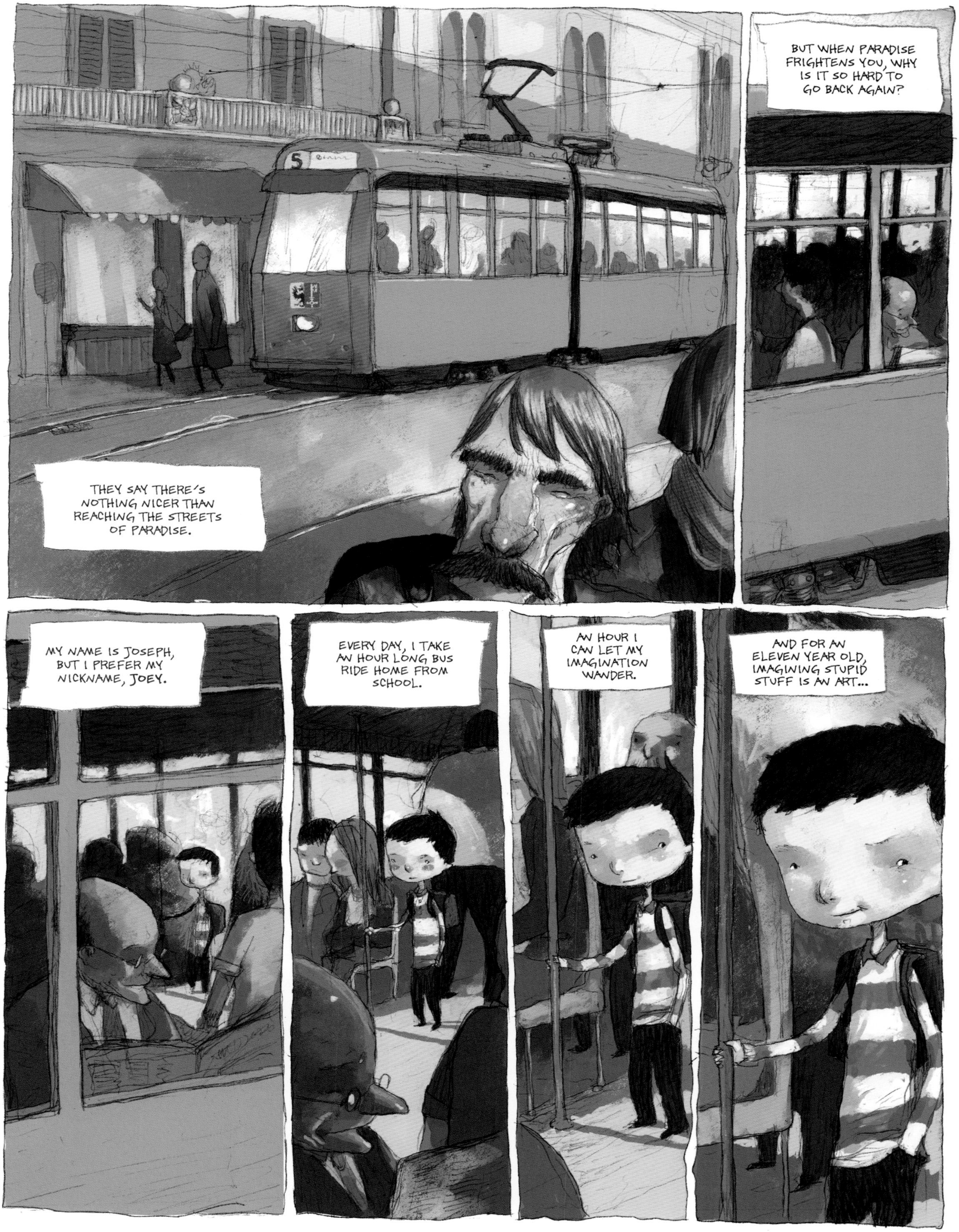
THEY SAY THERE'S NOTHING NICER THAN REACHING THE STREETS OF PARADISE.
BUT WHEN PARADISE FRIGHTENS YOU, WHY IS IT SO HARD TO GO BACK AGAIN?
MY NAME IS JOSEPH, BUT I PREFER MY NICKNAME, JOEY.
EVERY DAY, I TAKE AN HOUR LONG BUS RIDE HOME FROM SCHOOL.
AN HOUR I CAN LET MY IMAGINATION WANDER.
AND FOR AN ELEVEN YEAR OLD, IMAGINING STUPID STUFF IS AN ART...

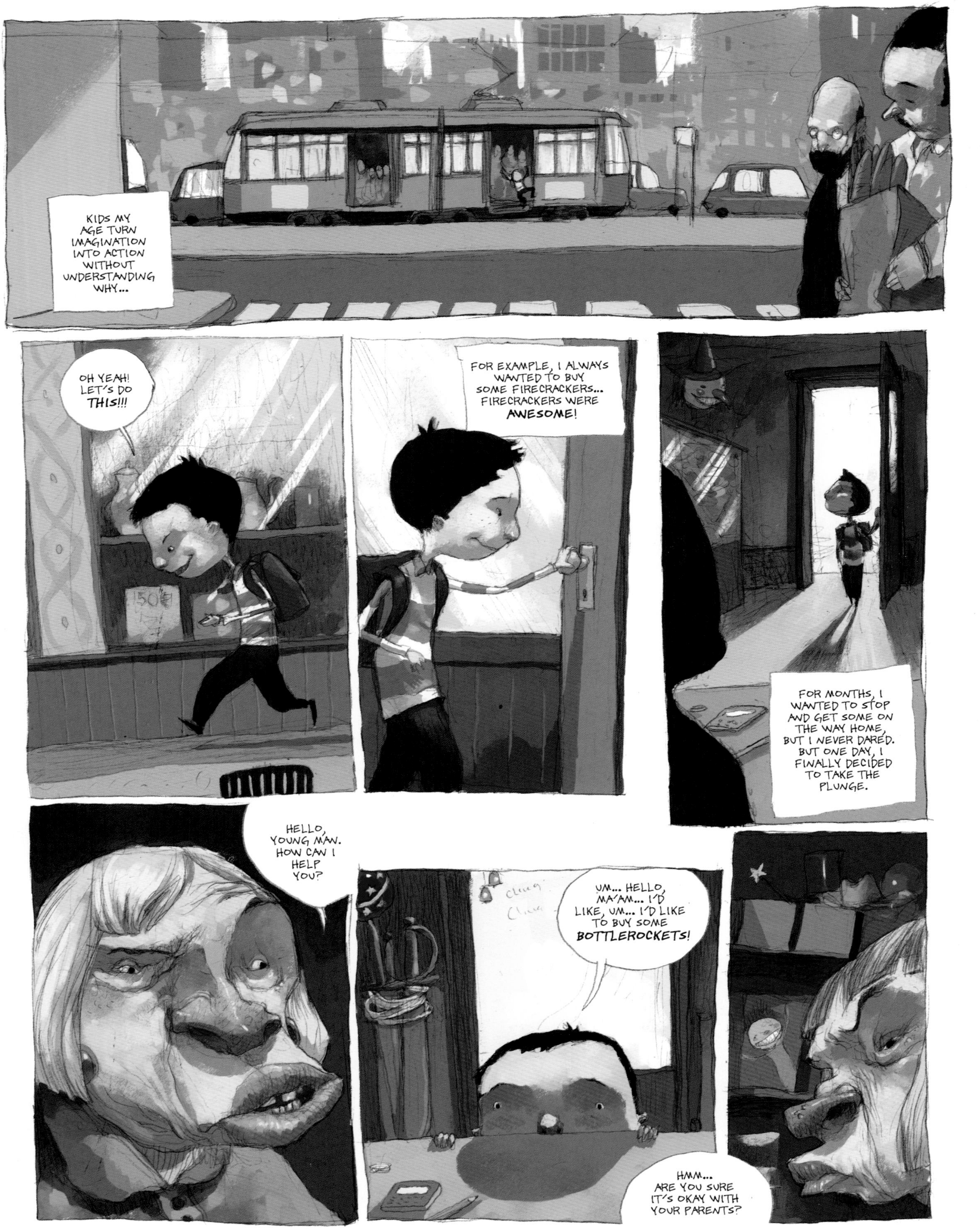
KIDS MY AGE TURN IMAGINATION INTO ACTION WITHOUT UNDERSTANDING WHY...
OH YEAH! LET'S DO THIS!!!
FOR EXAMPLE, I ALWAYS WANTED TO BUY SOME FIRECRACKERS... FIRECRACKERS WERE AWESOME!
FOR MONTHS, I WANTED TO STOP AND GET SOME ON THE WAY HOME, BUT I NEVER DARED. BUT ONE DAY, I FINALLY DECIDED TO TAKE THE PLUNGE.
HELLO, YOUNG MAN. HOW CAN I HELP YOU?
UM... HELLO, MA'AM... I'D LIKE, UM... I'D LIKE TO BUY SOME BOTTLEROCKETS!
HMM... ARE YOU SURE IT'S OKAY WITH YOUR PARENTS?

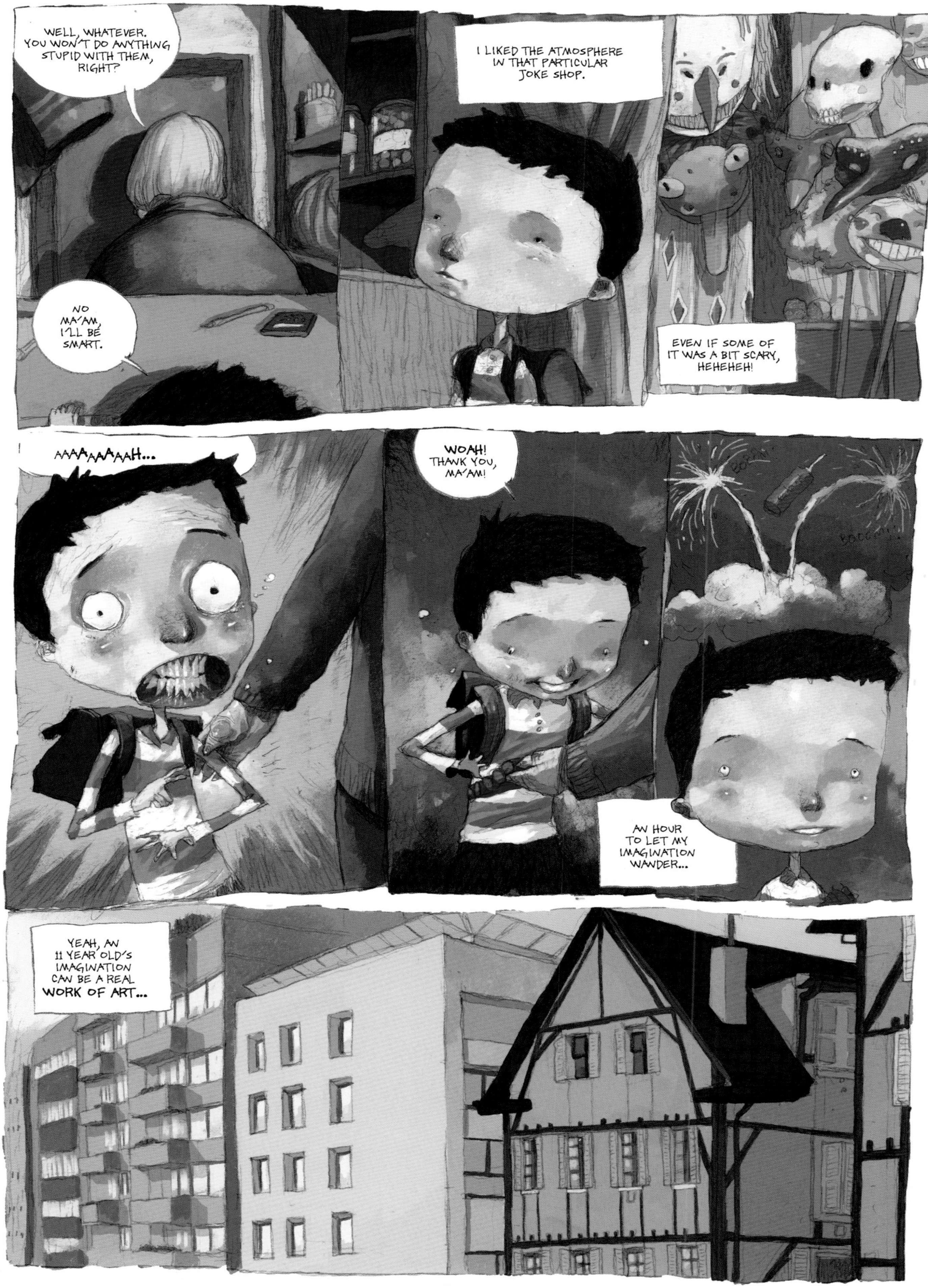
WELL, WHATEVER. YOU WON'T DO ANYTHING STUPID WITH THEM, RIGHT?
NO MA'AM, I'LL BE SMART.
I LIKED THE ATMOSPHERE IN THAT PARTICULAR JOKE SHOP.
EVEN IF SOME OF IT WAS A BIT SCARY, HEHEHEH!
AAAAAAAAH...
WOAH! THANK YOU, MA'AM!
AN HOUR TO LET MY IMAGINATION WANDER...
YEAH, AN 11 YEAR OLD'S IMAGINATION CAN BE A REAL WORK OF ART...

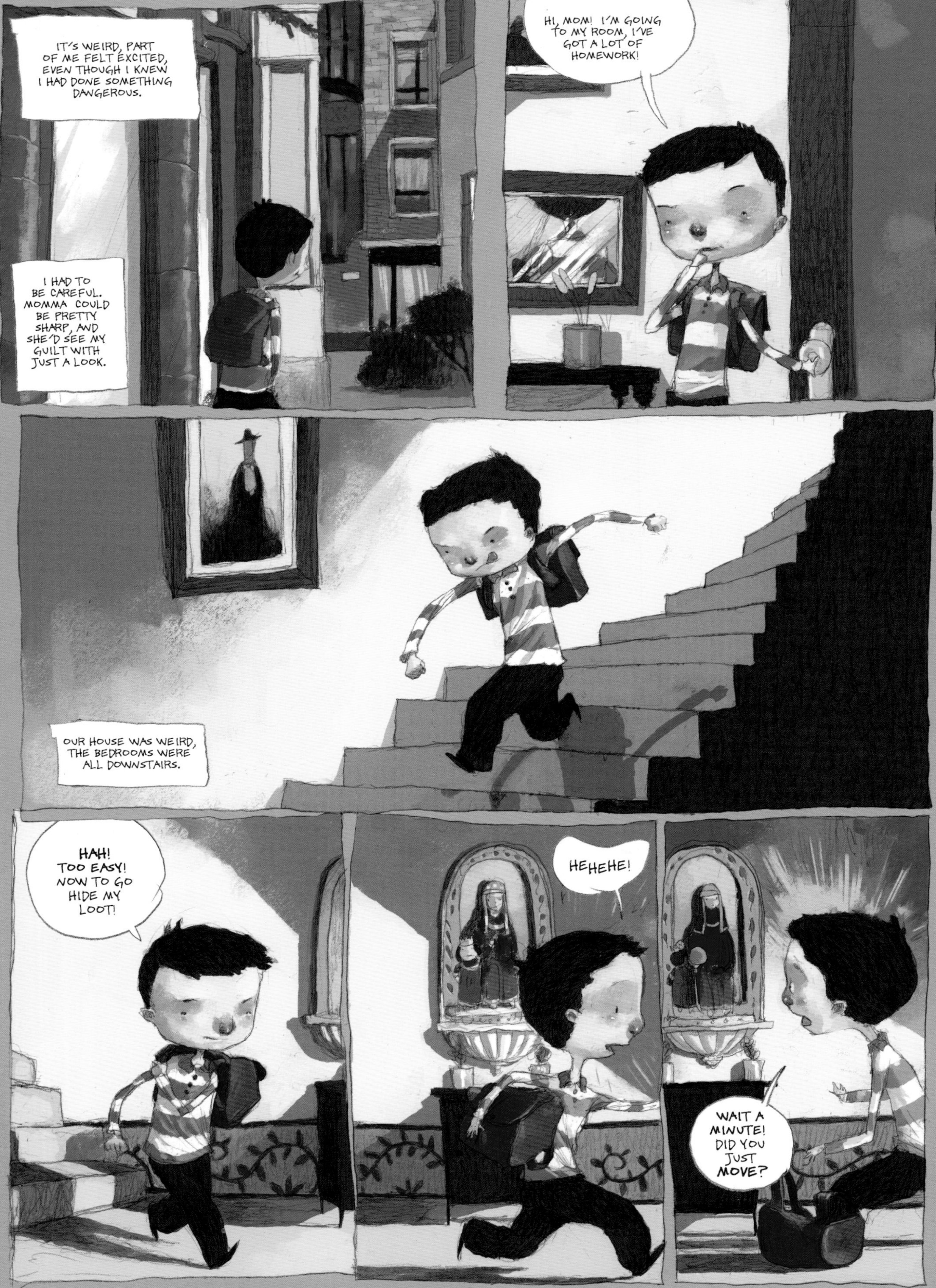
IT'S WEIRD, PART OF ME FELT EXCITED, EVEN THOUGH I KNEW I HAD DONE SOMETHING DANGEROUS.
I HAD TO BE CAREFUL. MOMMA COULD BE PRETTY SHARP, AND SHE'D SEE MY GUILT WITH JUST A LOOK.
HI, MOM! I'M GOING TO MY ROOM, I'VE GOT A LOT OF HOMEWORK!
OUR HOUSE WAS WEIRD, THE BEDROOMS WERE ALL DOWNSTAIRS.
HAH! TOO EASY! NOW TO GO HIDE MY LOOT!
HEHEHE!
WAIT A MINUTE! DID YOU JUST MOVE?

IN THE CORNER OF THE LIVING ROOM WAS A STATUE OF MARY AND THE HOLY CHILD.

NO WAY.... I'M SEEING THINGS...!

EVEN THOUGH I NEVER WENT TO SUNDAY SCHOOL, I WAS ALWAYS FASCINATED BY THIS STATUE.

HEY WAIT! DON'T BE AFRAID!

BUT RIGHT THEN, THE HOLY CHILD DISAPPEARED. I WITNESSED A SUPERNATURAL PHENOMENON!

WAIT, COME BACK! TALK TO ME!

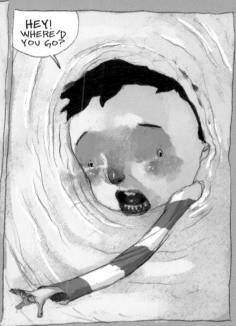

HEY! WHERE'D YOU GO?

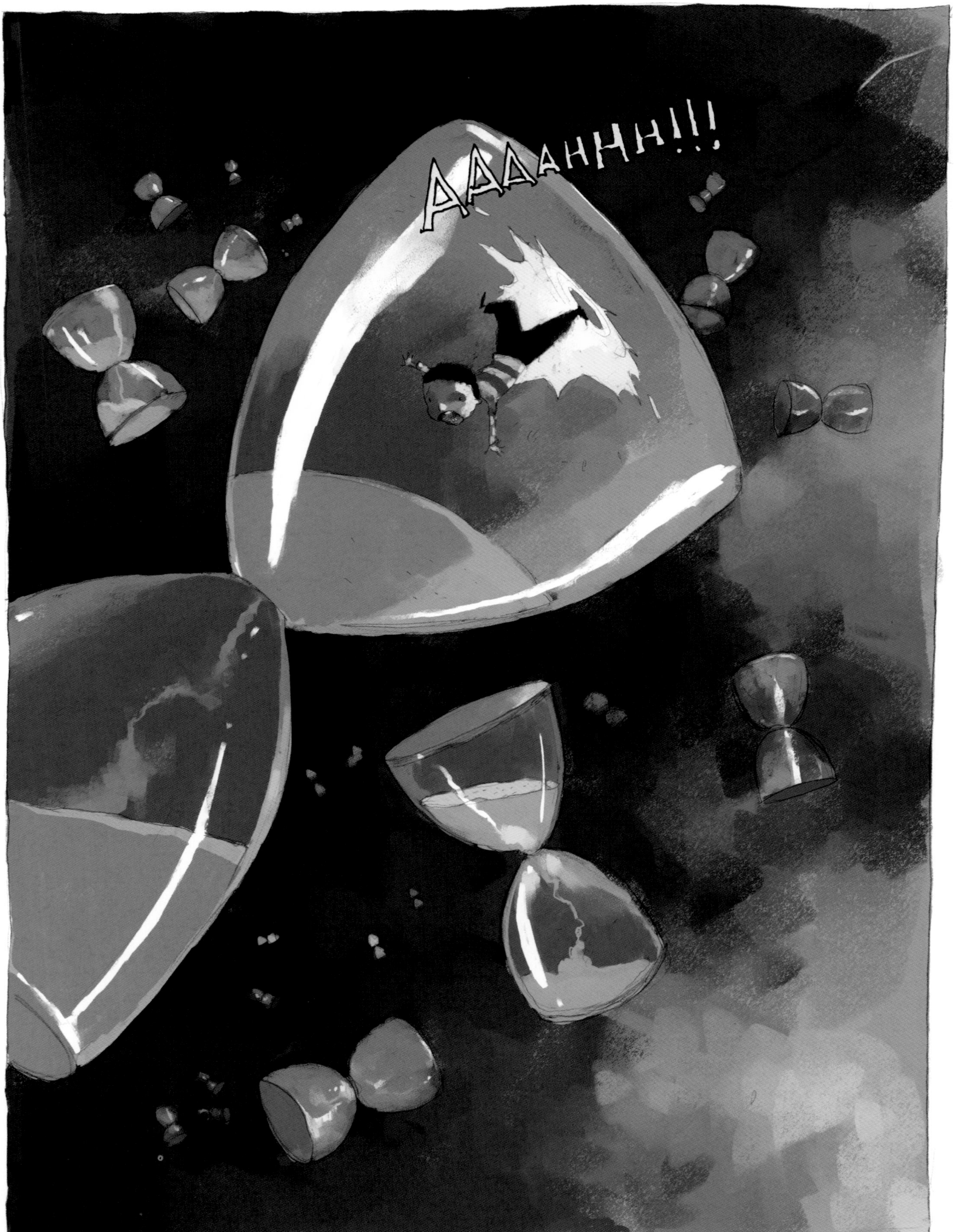
AAAAHHHH!!!

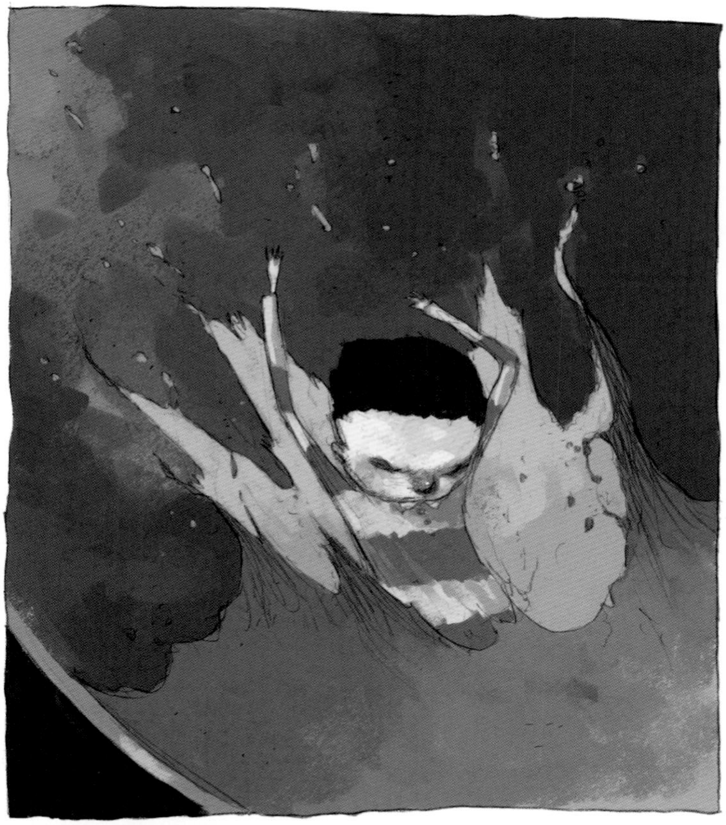

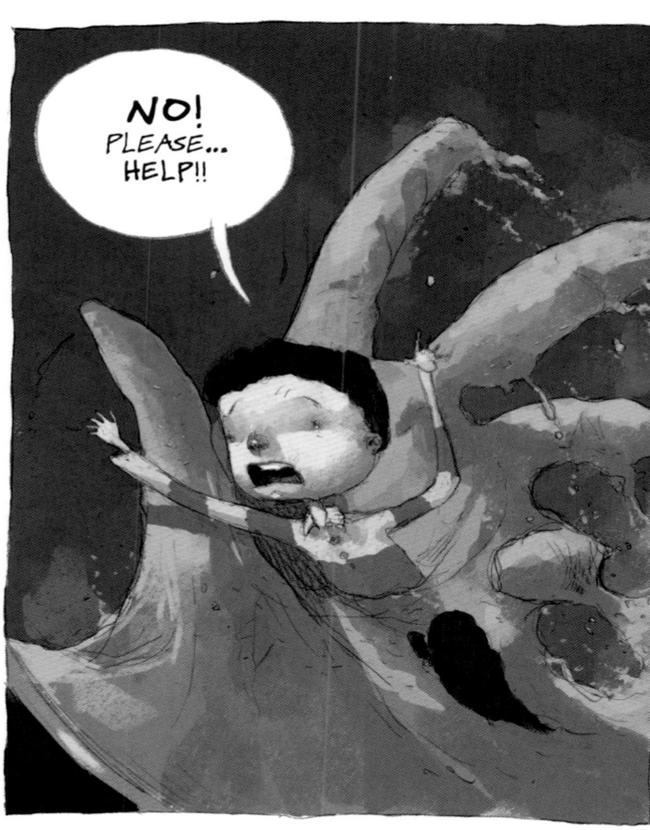
NO!
PLEASE...
HELP!!

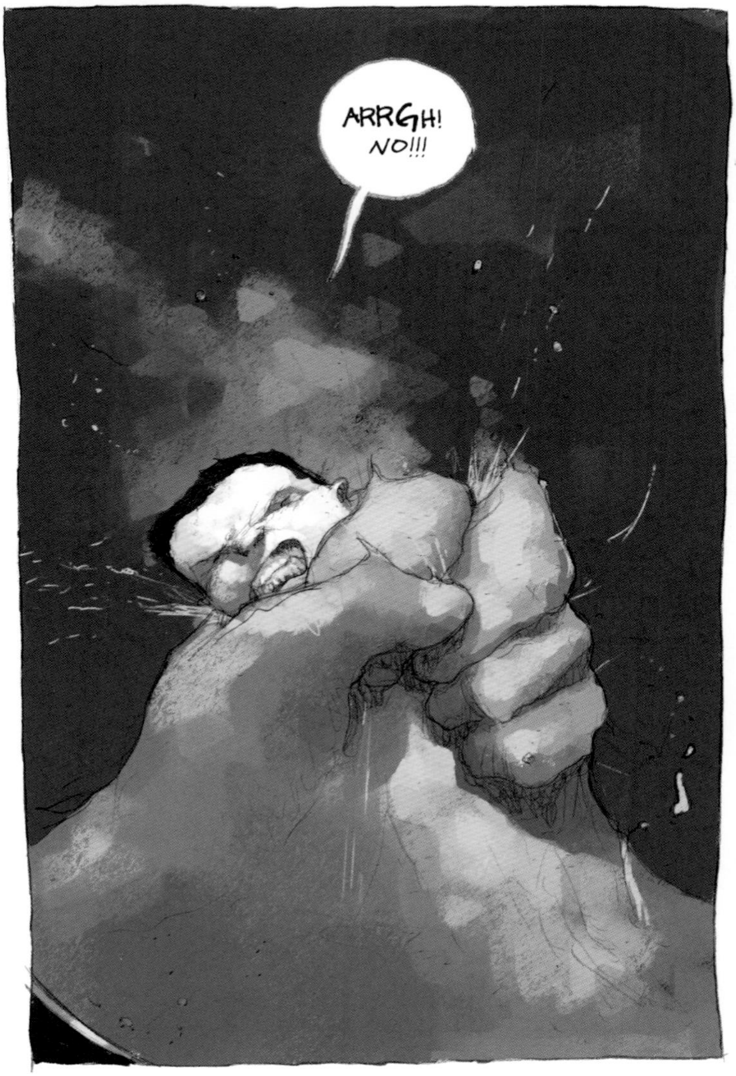
ARRGH!
NO!!!

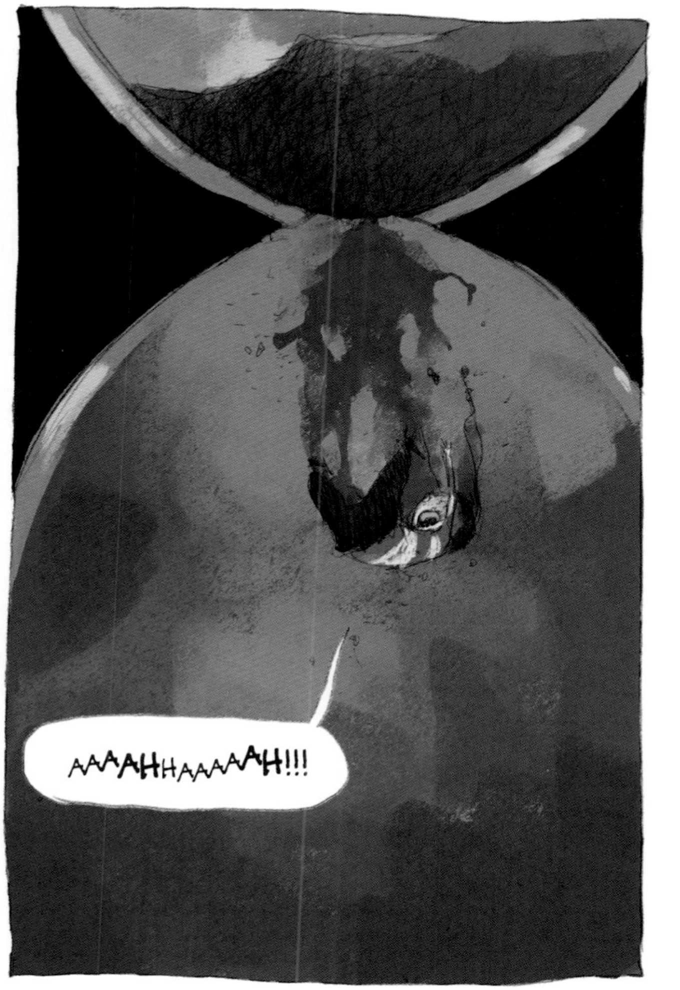
AAAAHHAAAAAH!!!

PLONG!

OWWW...

IT WAS LIKE A NIGHTMARE...

MOM! CAN YOU COME IN HERE??

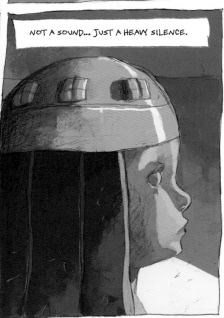

NOT A SOUND... JUST A HEAVY SILENCE.

BUT WHAT SEEMED LIKE A NIGHTMARE TURNED OUT TO BE A VERY REAL HELL...

POC!

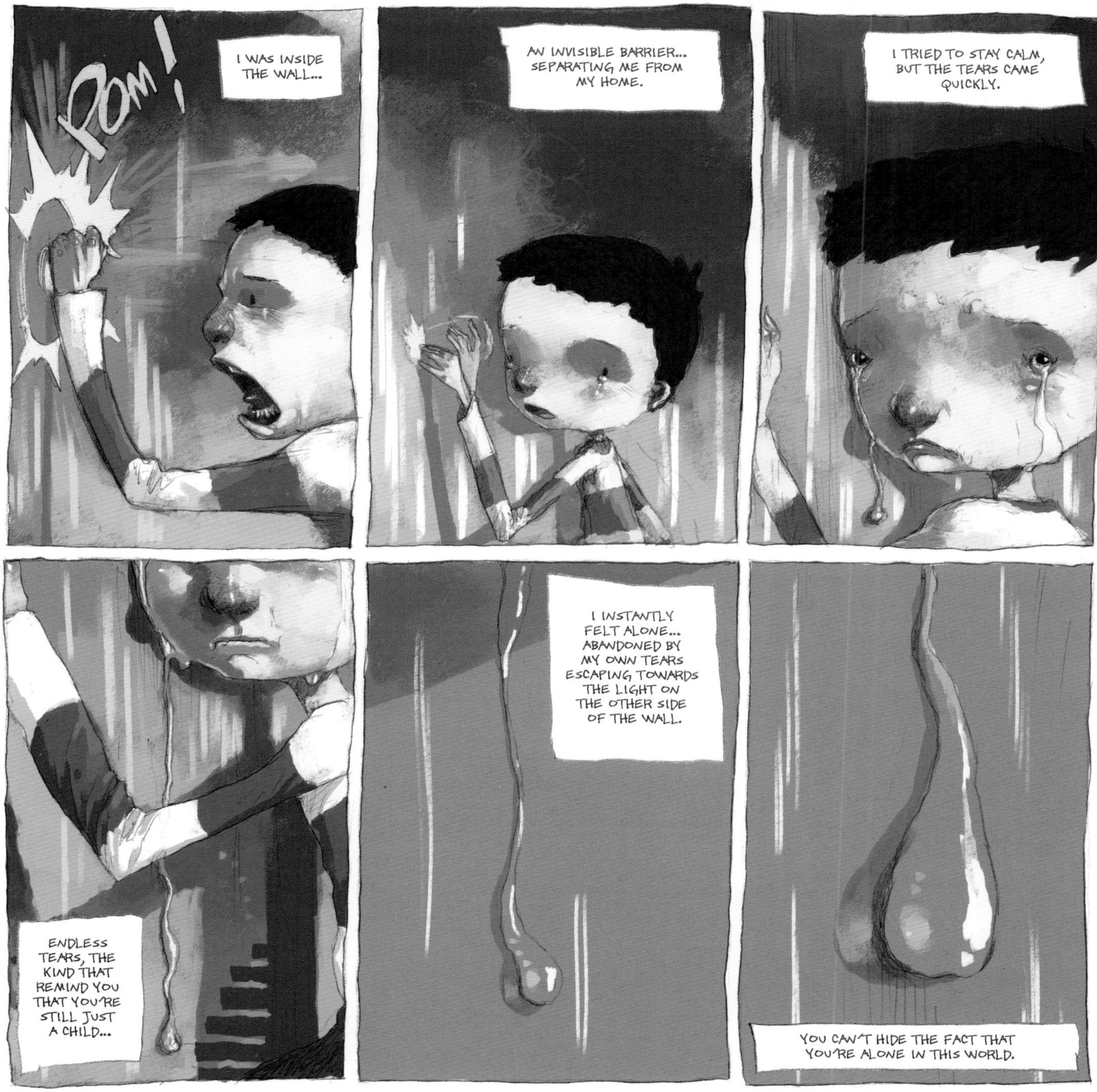
POM!
I WAS INSIDE THE WALL...
AN INVISIBLE BARRIER... SEPARATING ME FROM MY HOME.
I TRIED TO STAY CALM, BUT THE TEARS CAME QUICKLY.
ENDLESS TEARS, THE KIND THAT REMIND YOU THAT YOU'RE STILL JUST A CHILD...
I INSTANTLY FELT ALONE... ABANDONED BY MY OWN TEARS ESCAPING TOWARDS THE LIGHT ON THE OTHER SIDE OF THE WALL.
YOU CAN'T HIDE THE FACT THAT YOU'RE ALONE IN THIS WORLD.

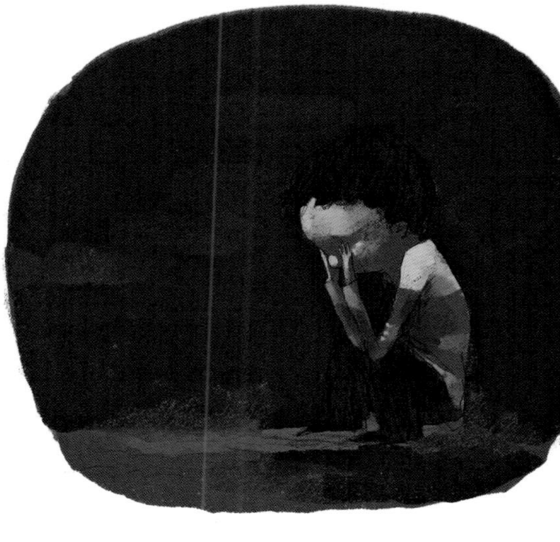

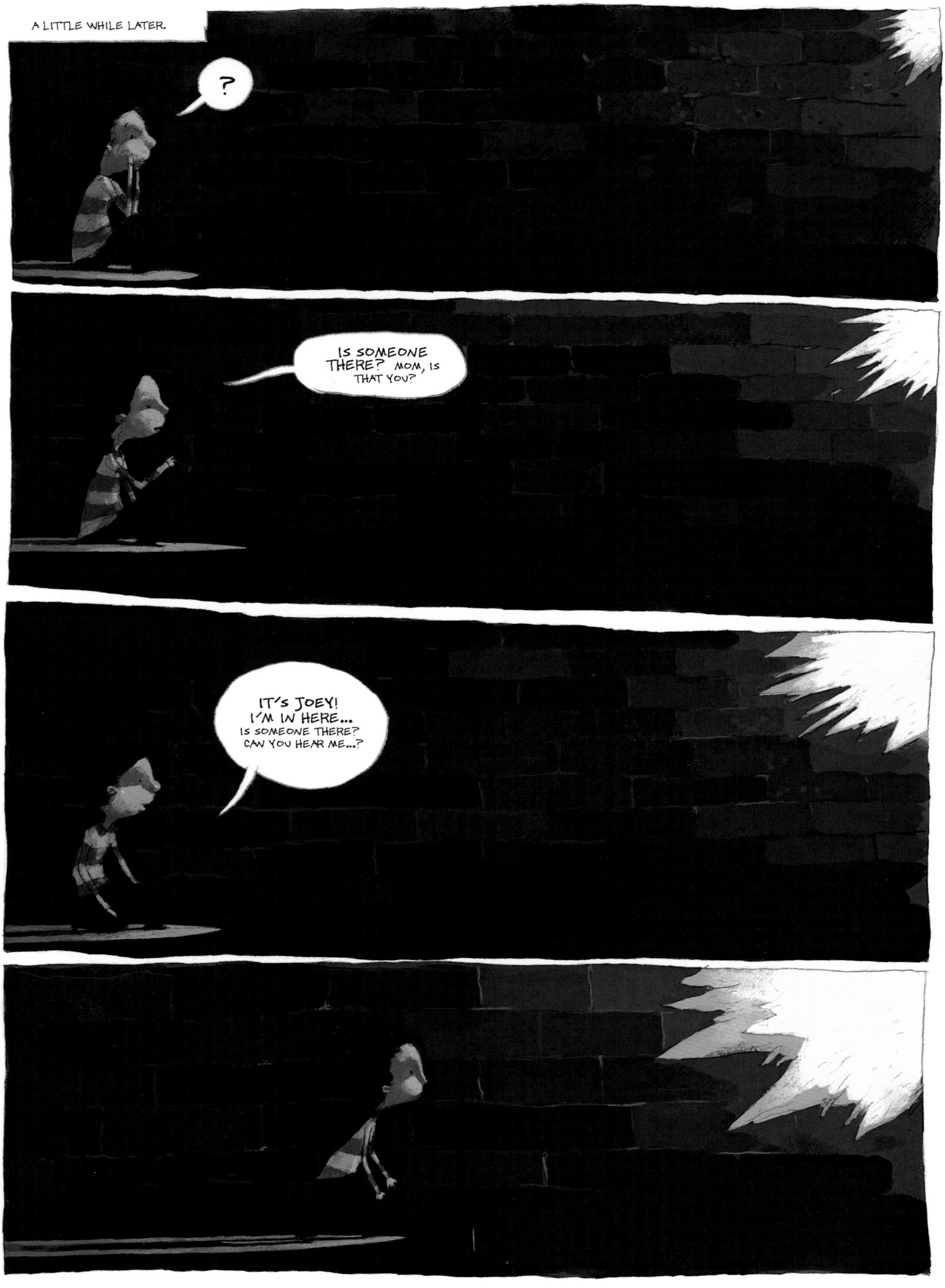
A LITTLE WHILE LATER.
?
IS SOMEONE THERE? MOM, IS THAT YOU?
IT'S JOEY! I'M IN HERE... IS SOMEONE THERE? CAN YOU HEAR ME...?

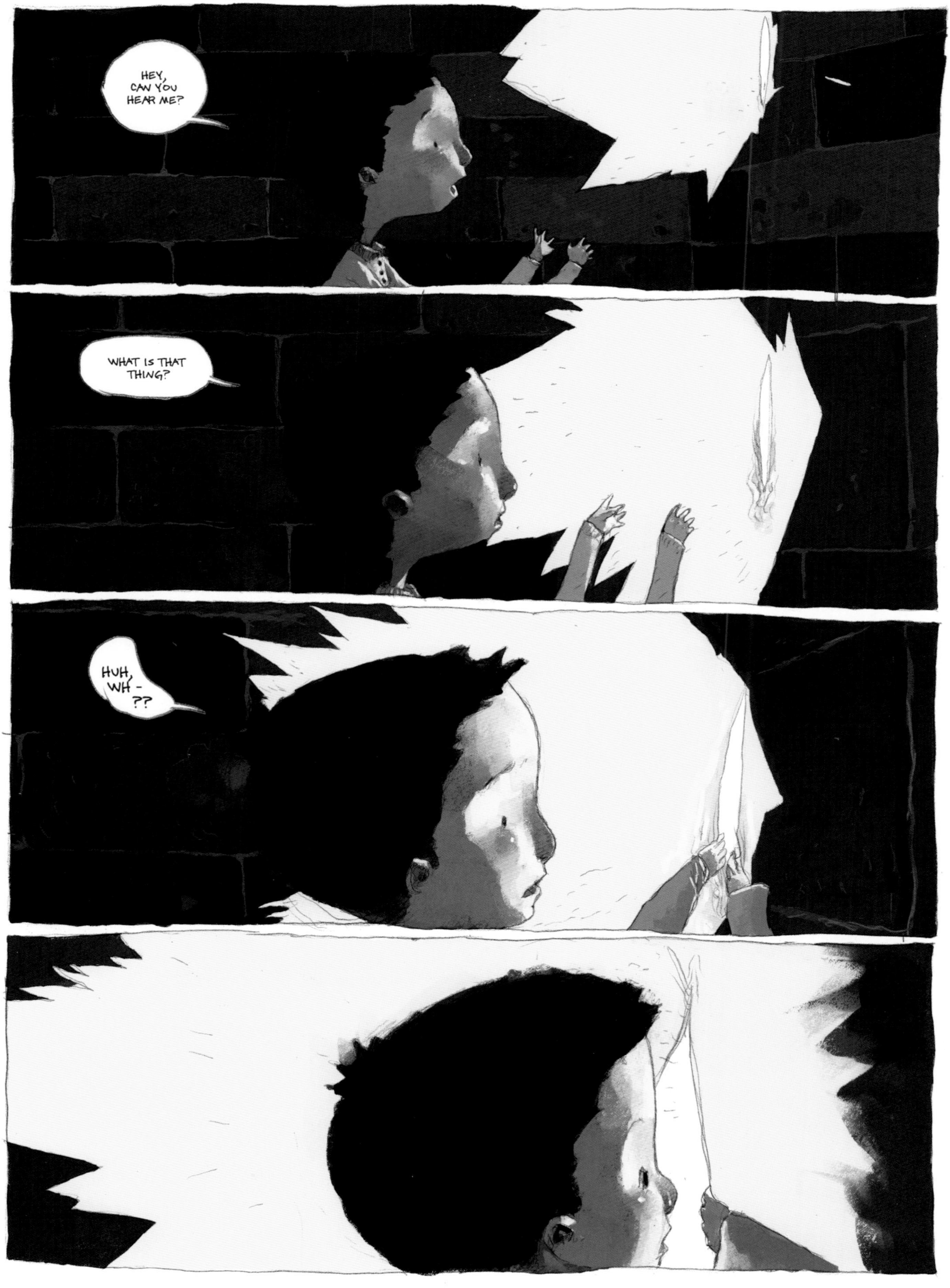
HEY, CAN YOU HEAR ME?
WHAT IS THAT THING?
HUH, WH- ??

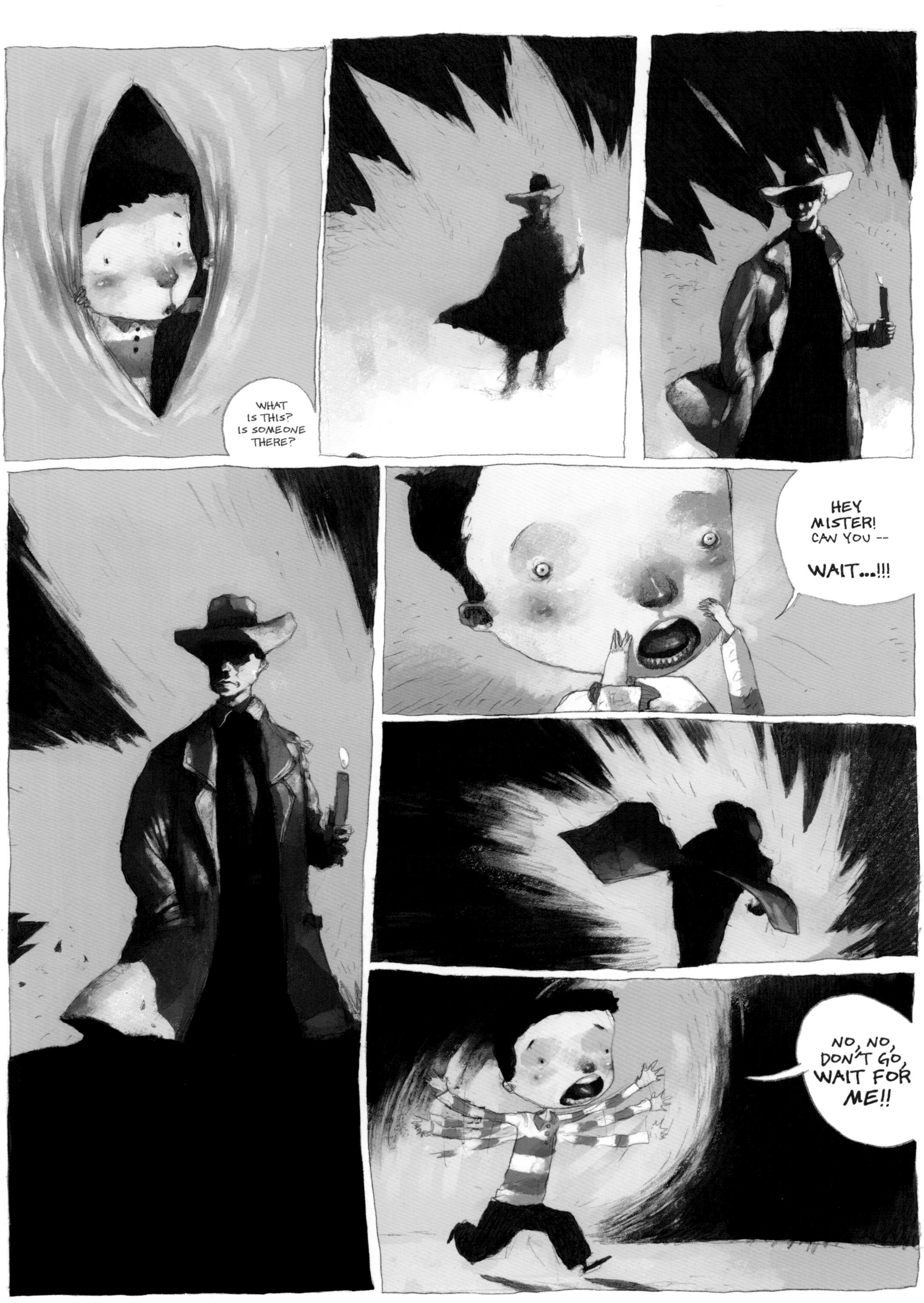
WHAT IS THIS? IS SOMEONE THERE?
HEY MISTER! CAN YOU --
WAIT...!!!
NO, NO, DON'T GO, WAIT FOR ME!!

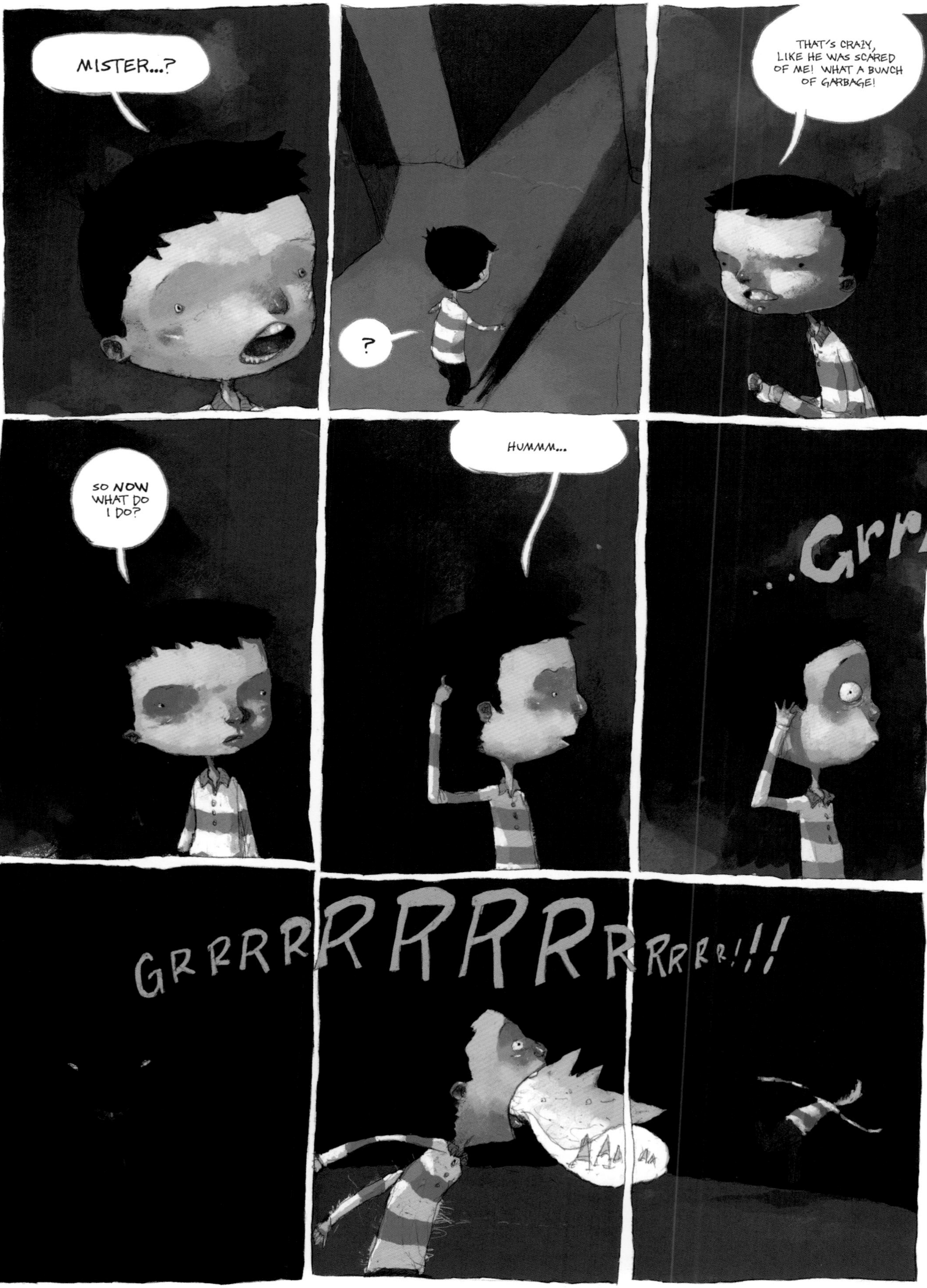
MISTER...?
?
THAT'S CRAZY, LIKE HE WAS SCARED OF ME! WHAT A BUNCH OF GARBAGE!
SO NOW WHAT DO I DO?
HUMMM...
...Grr
GRRRRRRRRRRRRRRR!!!

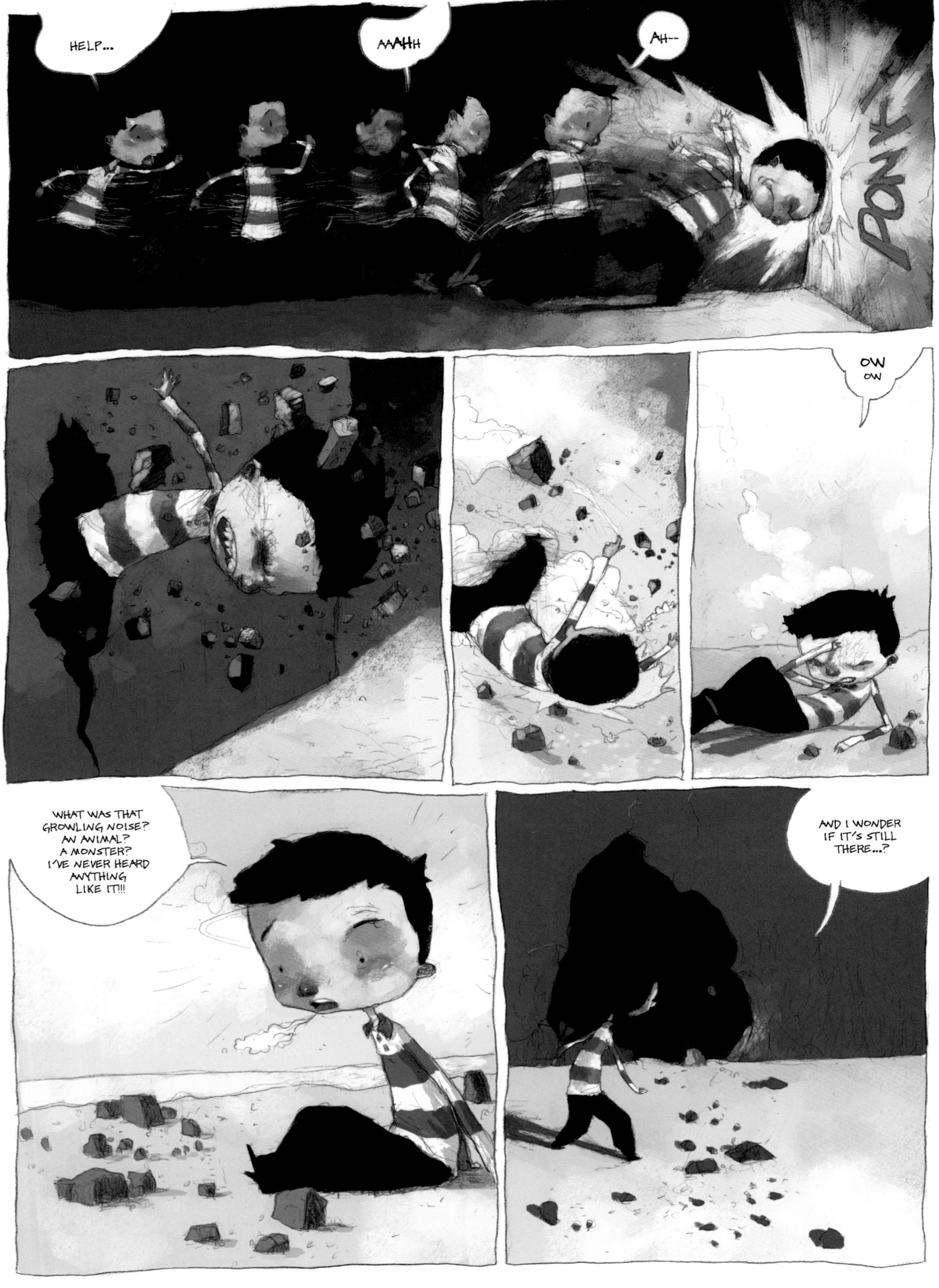
HELP...
AAAHH
AH--
PONK
OW
OW
WHAT WAS THAT GROWLING NOISE? AN ANIMAL? A MONSTER? I'VE NEVER HEARD ANYTHING LIKE IT!!!
AND I WONDER IF IT'S STILL THERE...?

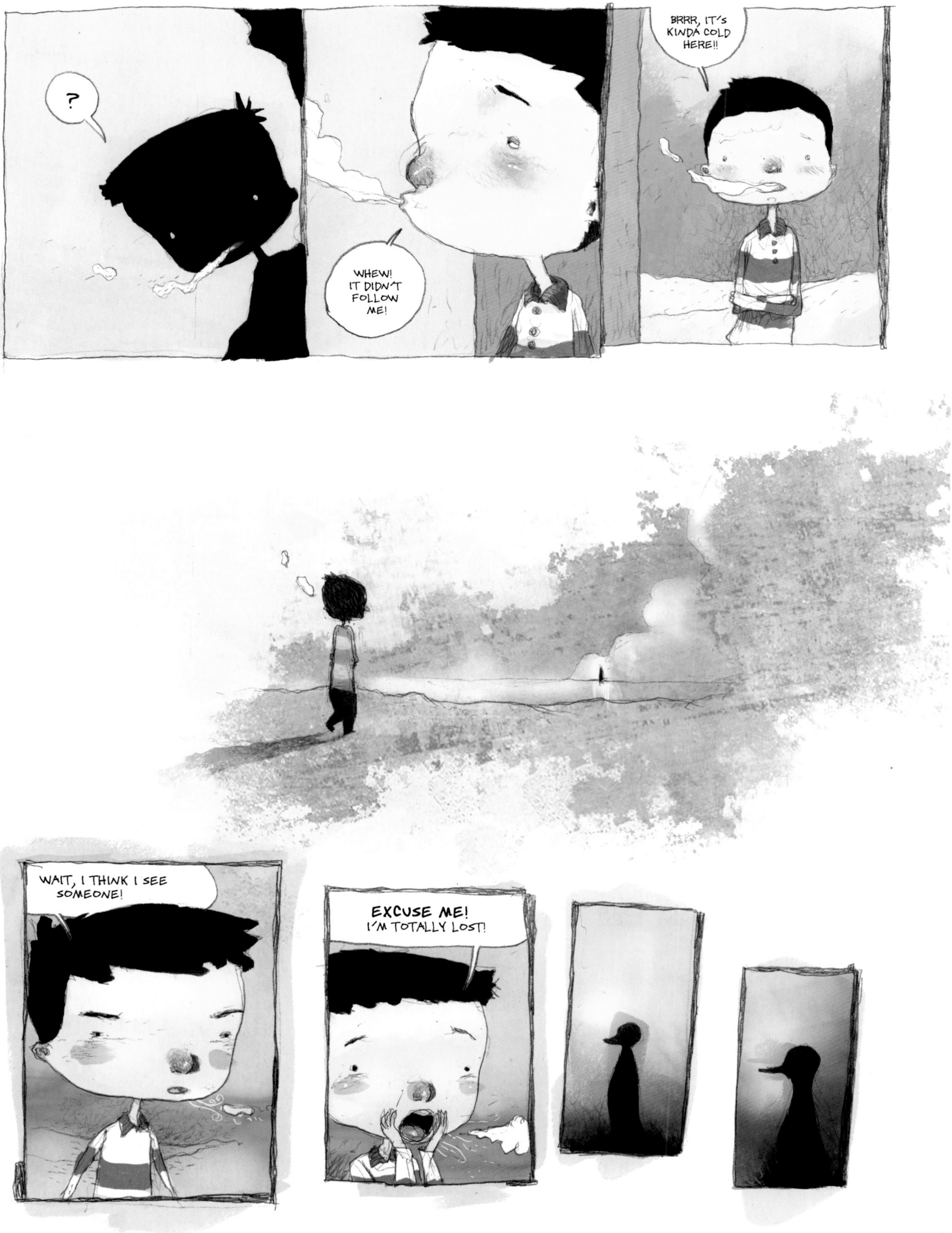
?
WHEW! IT DIDN'T FOLLOW ME!
BRRR, IT'S KINDA COLD HERE!!
WAIT, I THINK I SEE SOMEONE!
EXCUSE ME! I'M TOTALLY LOST!

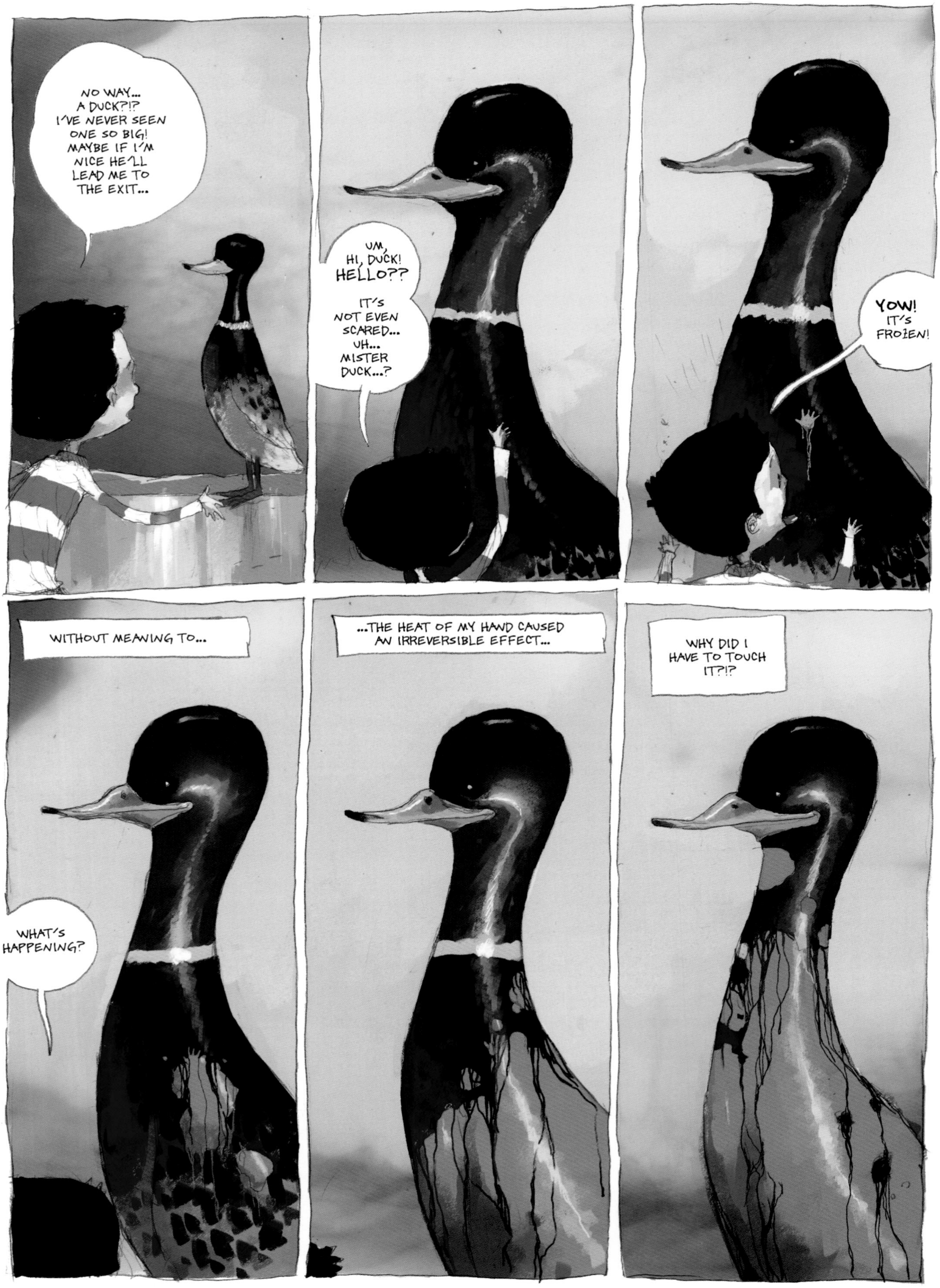
NO WAY... A DUCK?!? I'VE NEVER SEEN ONE SO BIG! MAYBE IF I'M NICE HE'LL LEAD ME TO THE EXIT...
UM, HI, DUCK! HELLO??
IT'S NOT EVEN SCARED... UH... MISTER DUCK...?
YOW! IT'S FROZEN!
WITHOUT MEANING TO...
WHAT'S HAPPENING?
...THE HEAT OF MY HAND CAUSED AN IRREVERSIBLE EFFECT...
WHY DID I HAVE TO TOUCH IT?!?

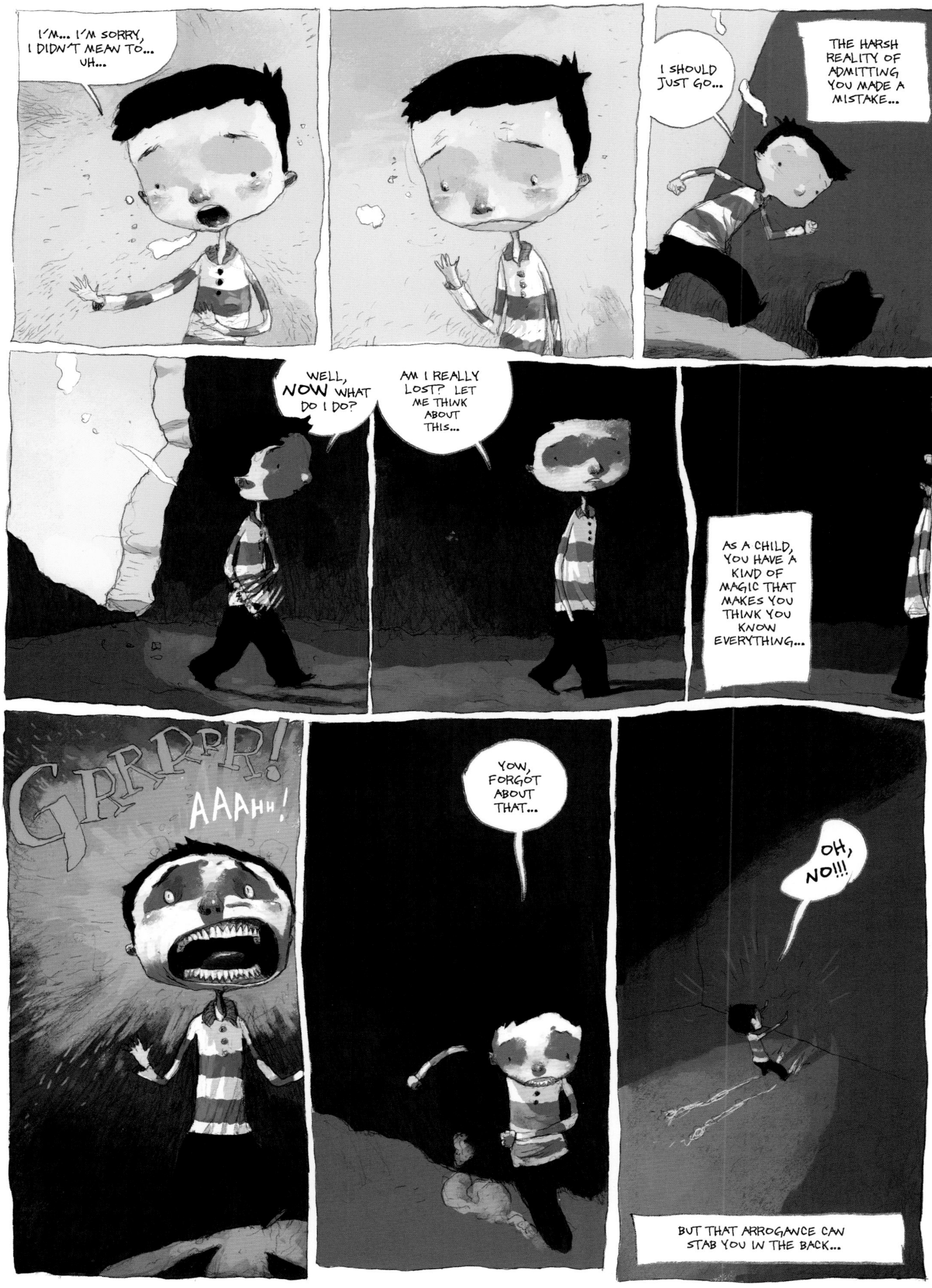
I'M... I'M SORRY, I DIDN'T MEAN TO... UH...
I SHOULD JUST GO...
THE HARSH REALITY OF ADMITTING YOU MADE A MISTAKE...
WELL, NOW WHAT DO I DO?
AM I REALLY LOST? LET ME THINK ABOUT THIS...
AS A CHILD, YOU HAVE A KIND OF MAGIC THAT MAKES YOU THINK YOU KNOW EVERYTHING...
GRRRRR!
AAAHH!
YOW, FORGOT ABOUT THAT...
OH, NO!!!
BUT THAT ARROGANCE CAN STAB YOU IN THE BACK...

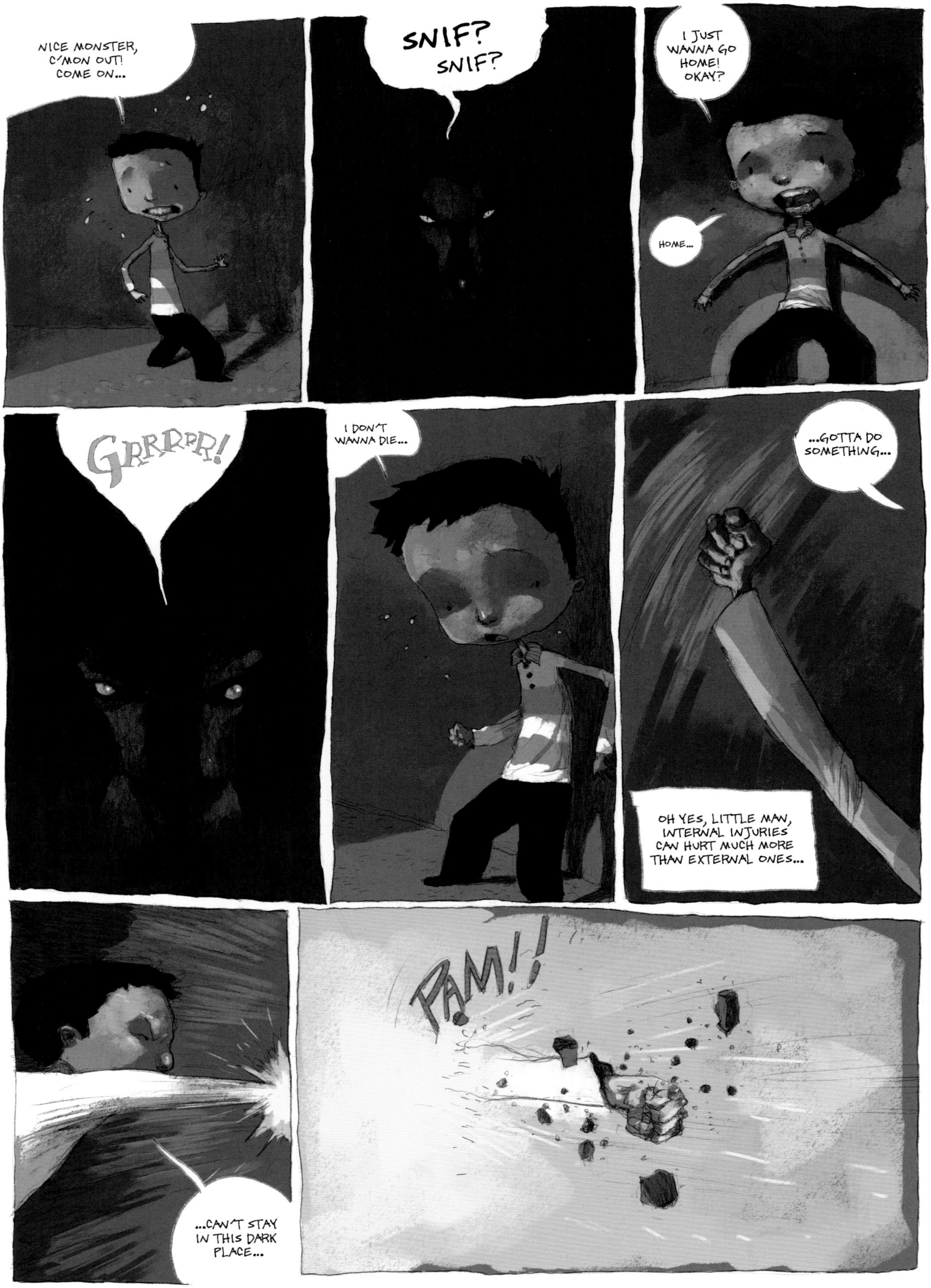
NICE MONSTER, C'MON OUT! COME ON...
SNIF? SNIF?
I JUST WANNA GO HOME! OKAY?
HOME...
GRRRRR!
I DON'T WANNA DIE...
...GOTTA DO SOMETHING...
OH YES, LITTLE MAN, INTERNAL INJURIES CAN HURT MUCH MORE THAN EXTERNAL ONES...
...CAN'T STAY IN THIS DARK PLACE...
PAM!!

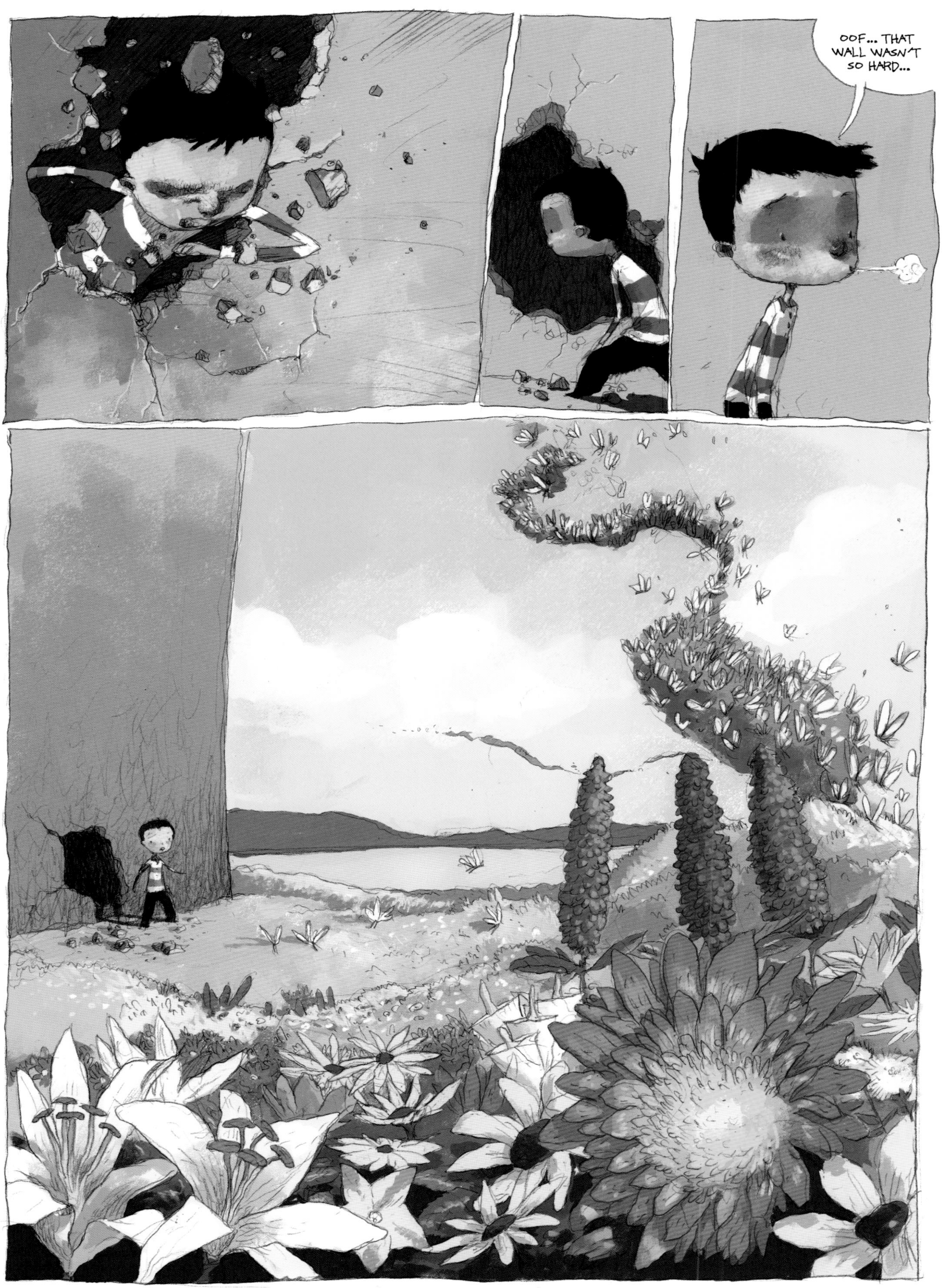
OOF... THAT WALL WASN'T SO HARD...

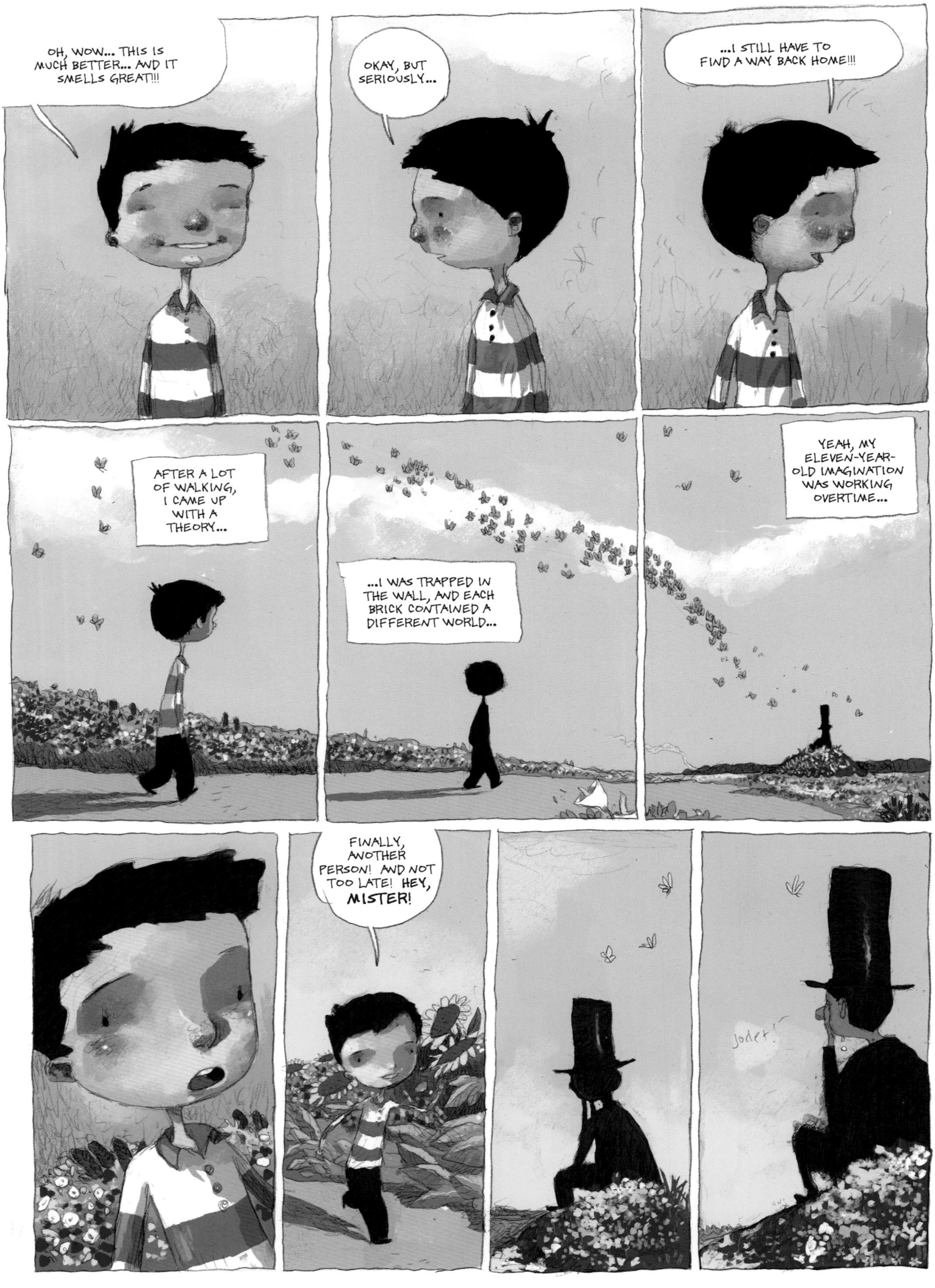
OH, WOW... THIS IS MUCH BETTER... AND IT SMELLS GREAT!!!
OKAY, BUT SERIOUSLY...
...I STILL HAVE TO FIND A WAY BACK HOME!!!
AFTER A LOT OF WALKING, I CAME UP WITH A THEORY...
...I WAS TRAPPED IN THE WALL, AND EACH BRICK CONTAINED A DIFFERENT WORLD...
YEAH, MY ELEVEN-YEAR-OLD IMAGINATION WAS WORKING OVERTIME...
FINALLY, ANOTHER PERSON! AND NOT TOO LATE! HEY, MISTER!
Joder!

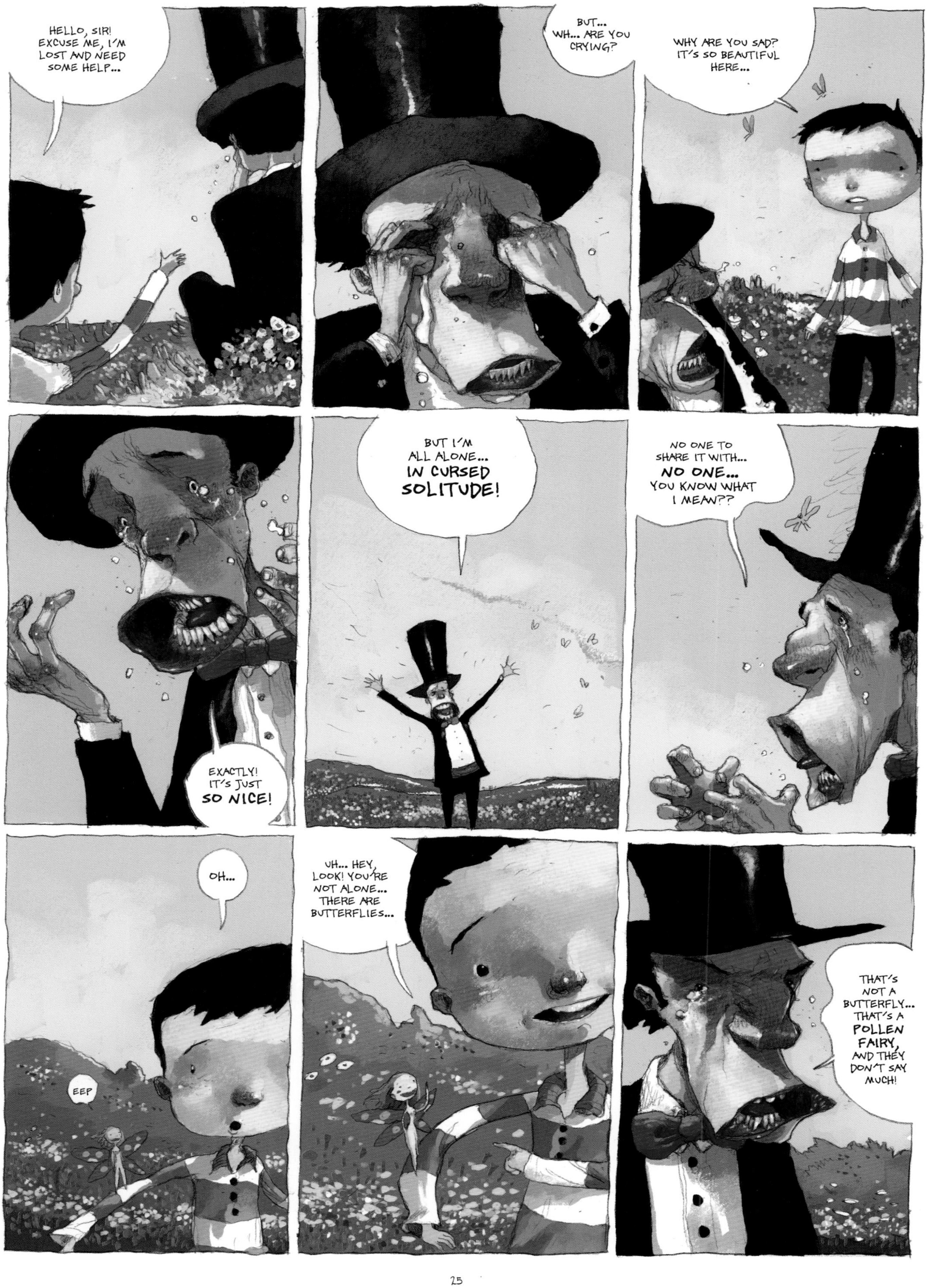
HELLO, SIR! EXCUSE ME, I'M LOST AND NEED SOME HELP...
BUT... WH... ARE YOU CRYING?
WHY ARE YOU SAD? IT'S SO BEAUTIFUL HERE...
EXACTLY! IT'S JUST SO NICE!
BUT I'M ALL ALONE... IN CURSED SOLITUDE!
NO ONE TO SHARE IT WITH... NO ONE... YOU KNOW WHAT I MEAN??
OH...
EEP
UH... HEY, LOOK! YOU'RE NOT ALONE... THERE ARE BUTTERFLIES...
THAT'S NOT A BUTTERFLY... THAT'S A POLLEN FAIRY, AND THEY DON'T SAY MUCH!

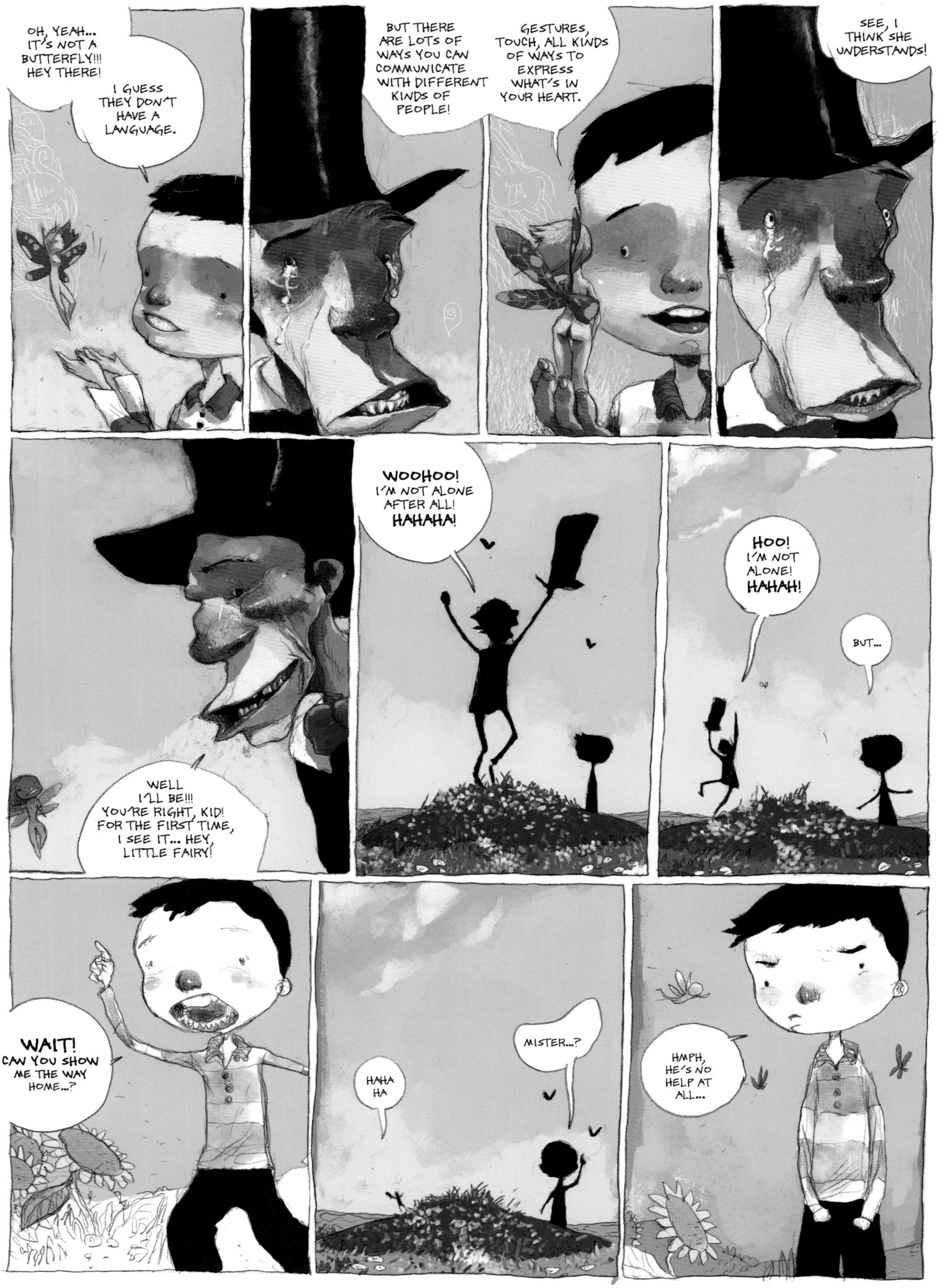
OH, YEAH... IT'S NOT A BUTTERFLY!!! HEY THERE!
I GUESS THEY DON'T HAVE A LANGUAGE.
BUT THERE ARE LOTS OF WAYS YOU CAN COMMUNICATE WITH DIFFERENT KINDS OF PEOPLE!
GESTURES, TOUCH, ALL KINDS OF WAYS TO EXPRESS WHAT'S IN YOUR HEART.
SEE, I THINK SHE UNDERSTANDS!
WELL I'LL BE!!! YOU'RE RIGHT, KID! FOR THE FIRST TIME, I SEE IT... HEY, LITTLE FAIRY!
WOOHOO! I'M NOT ALONE AFTER ALL! HAHAHA!
HOO! I'M NOT ALONE! HAHAH!
BUT...
WAIT! CAN YOU SHOW ME THE WAY HOME...?
HAHA HA
MISTER...?
HMPH, HE'S NO HELP AT ALL...

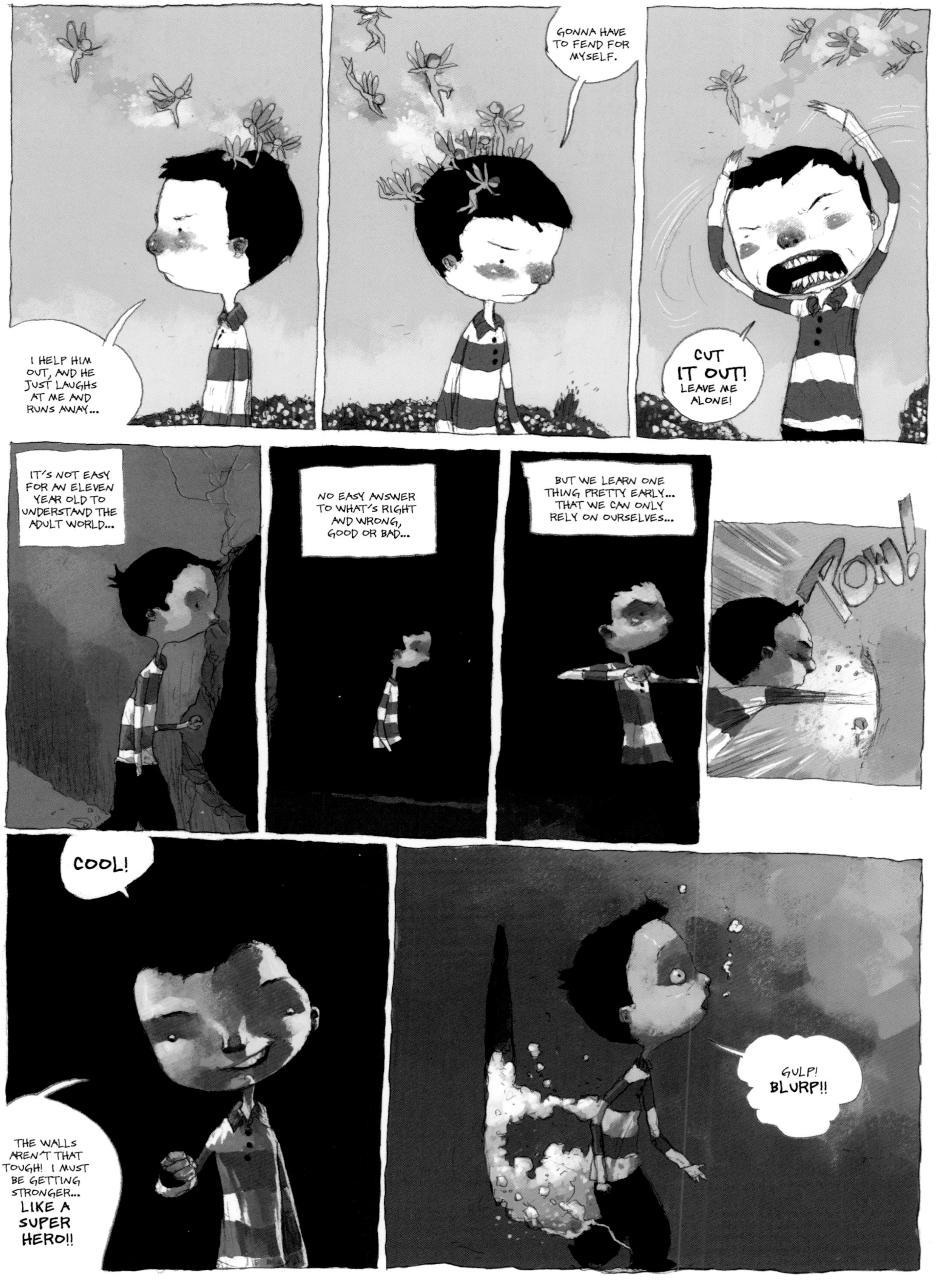
I HELP HIM OUT, AND HE JUST LAUGHS AT ME AND RUNS AWAY...
GONNA HAVE TO FEND FOR MYSELF.
CUT IT OUT! LEAVE ME ALONE!
IT'S NOT EASY FOR AN ELEVEN YEAR OLD TO UNDERSTAND THE ADULT WORLD...
NO EASY ANSWER TO WHAT'S RIGHT AND WRONG, GOOD OR BAD...
BUT WE LEARN ONE THING PRETTY EARLY... THAT WE CAN ONLY RELY ON OURSELVES...
POW!
COOL!
THE WALLS AREN'T THAT TOUGH! I MUST BE GETTING STRONGER... LIKE A SUPER HERO!!
GULP! BLURP!!

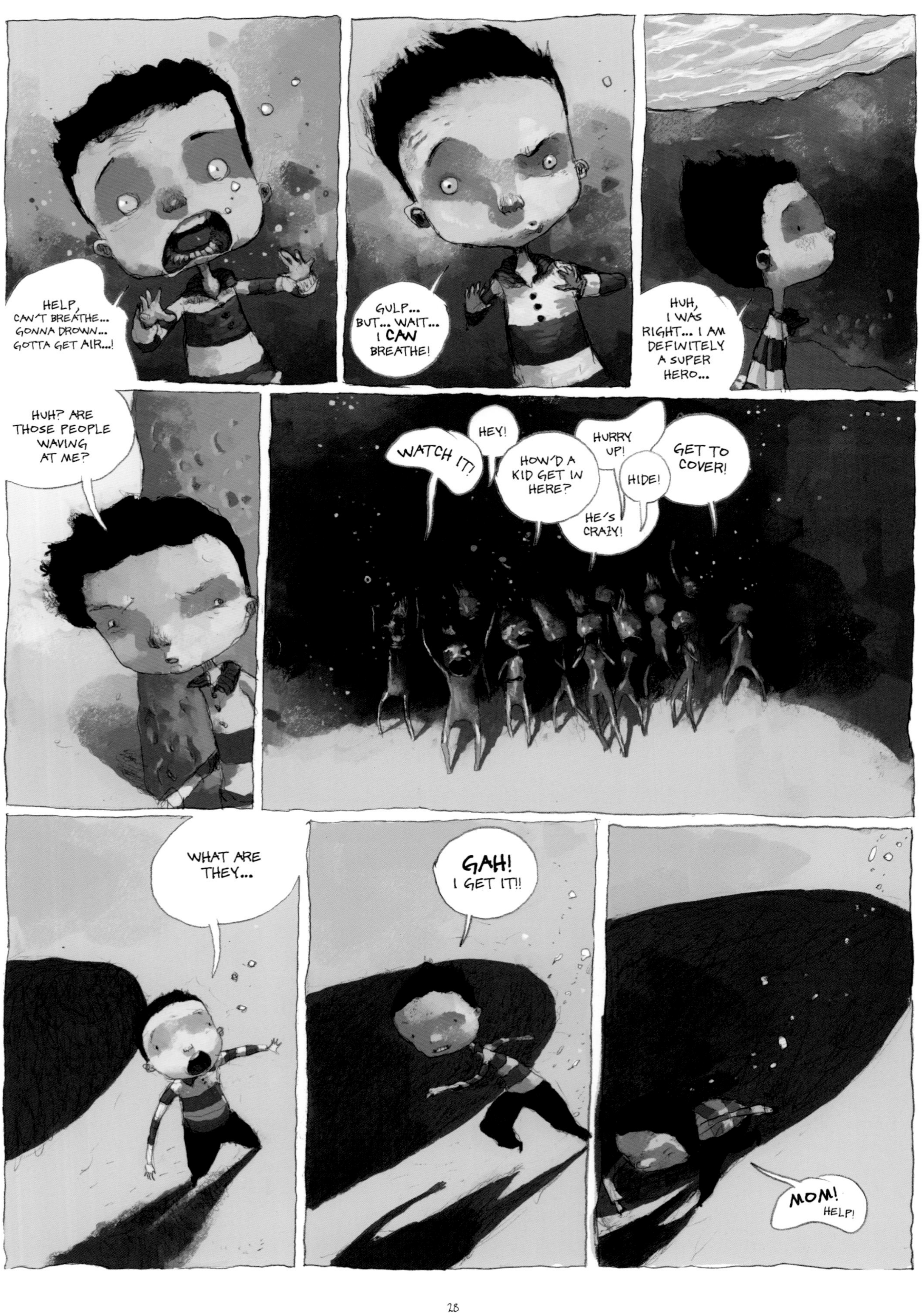
HELP, CAN'T BREATHE... GONNA DROWN... GOTTA GET AIR...!
GULP... BUT... WAIT... I CAN BREATHE!
HUH, I WAS RIGHT... I AM DEFINITELY A SUPER HERO...
HUH? ARE THOSE PEOPLE WAVING AT ME?
WATCH IT!
HEY!
HOW'D A KID GET IN HERE?
HURRY UP!
HIDE!
HE'S CRAZY!
GET TO COVER!
WHAT ARE THEY...
GAH! I GET IT!!
MOM! HELP!

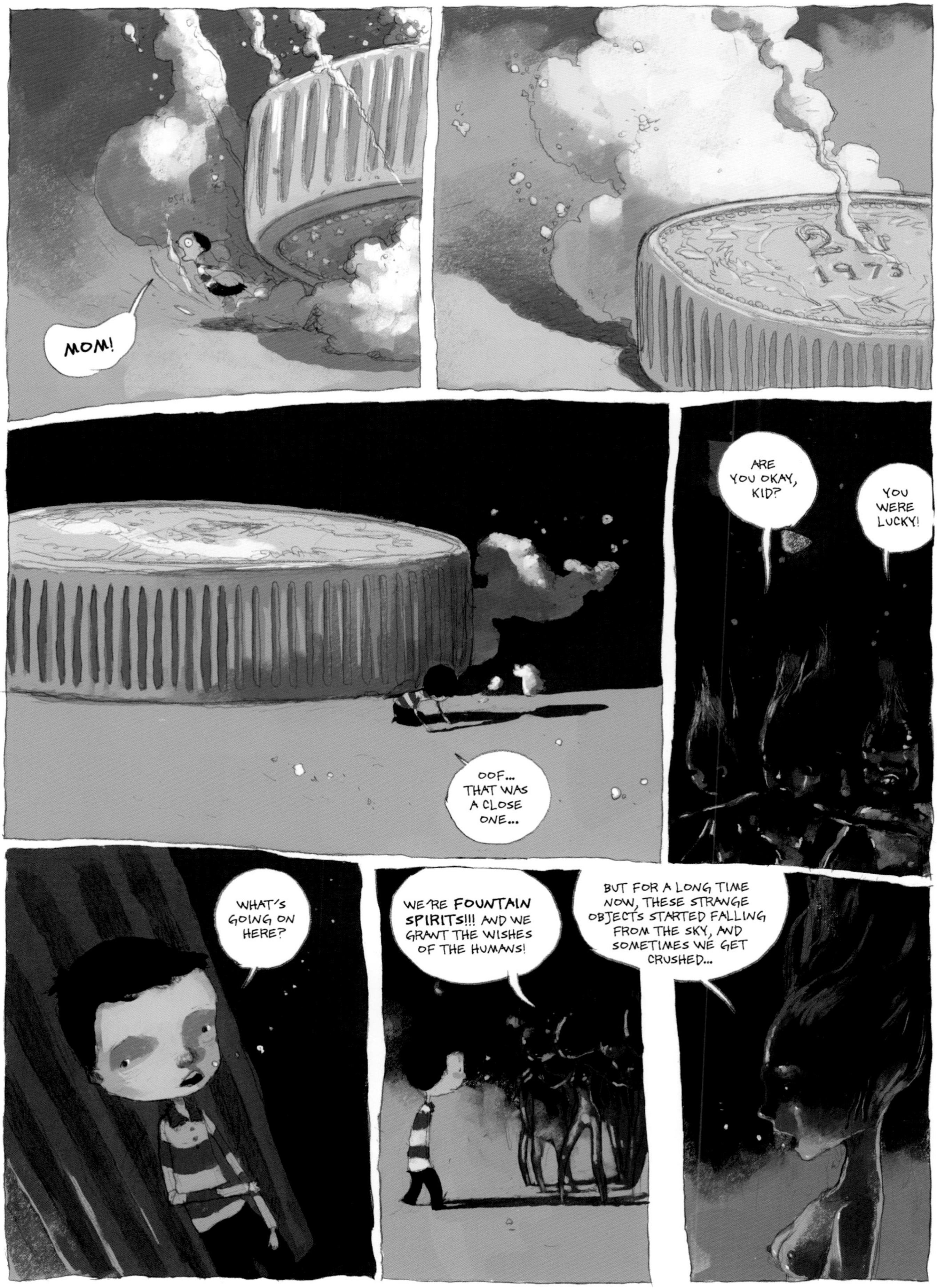
MOM!
1973
OOF... THAT WAS A CLOSE ONE...
ARE YOU OKAY, KID?
YOU WERE LUCKY!
WHAT'S GOING ON HERE?
WE'RE FOUNTAIN SPIRITS!!! AND WE GRANT THE WISHES OF THE HUMANS!
BUT FOR A LONG TIME NOW, THESE STRANGE OBJECTS STARTED FALLING FROM THE SKY, AND SOMETIMES WE GET CRUSHED...

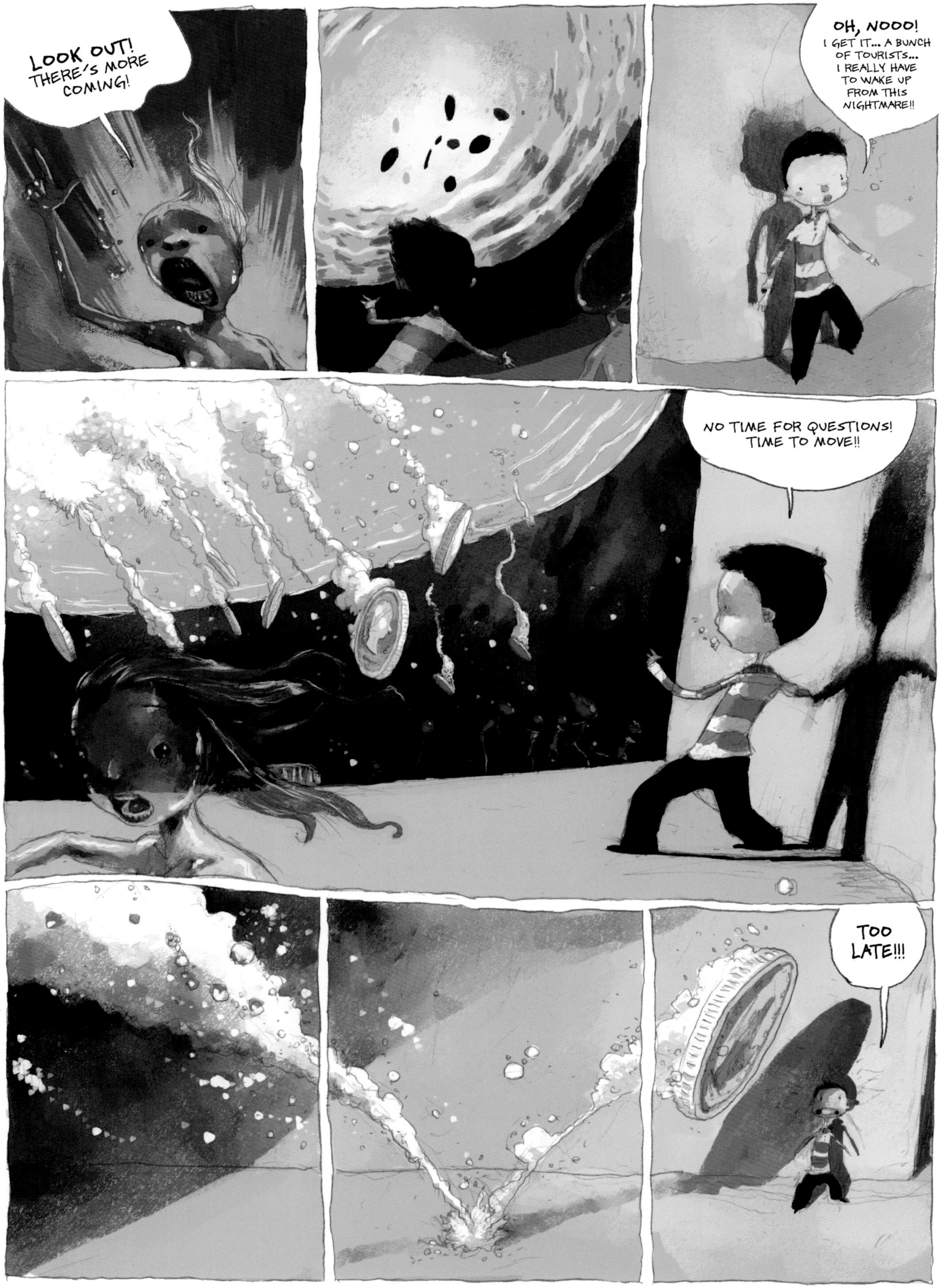
LOOK OUT! THERE'S MORE COMING!
OH, NOOO! I GET IT... A BUNCH OF TOURISTS... I REALLY HAVE TO WAKE UP FROM THIS NIGHTMARE!!
NO TIME FOR QUESTIONS! TIME TO MOVE!!
TOO LATE!!!

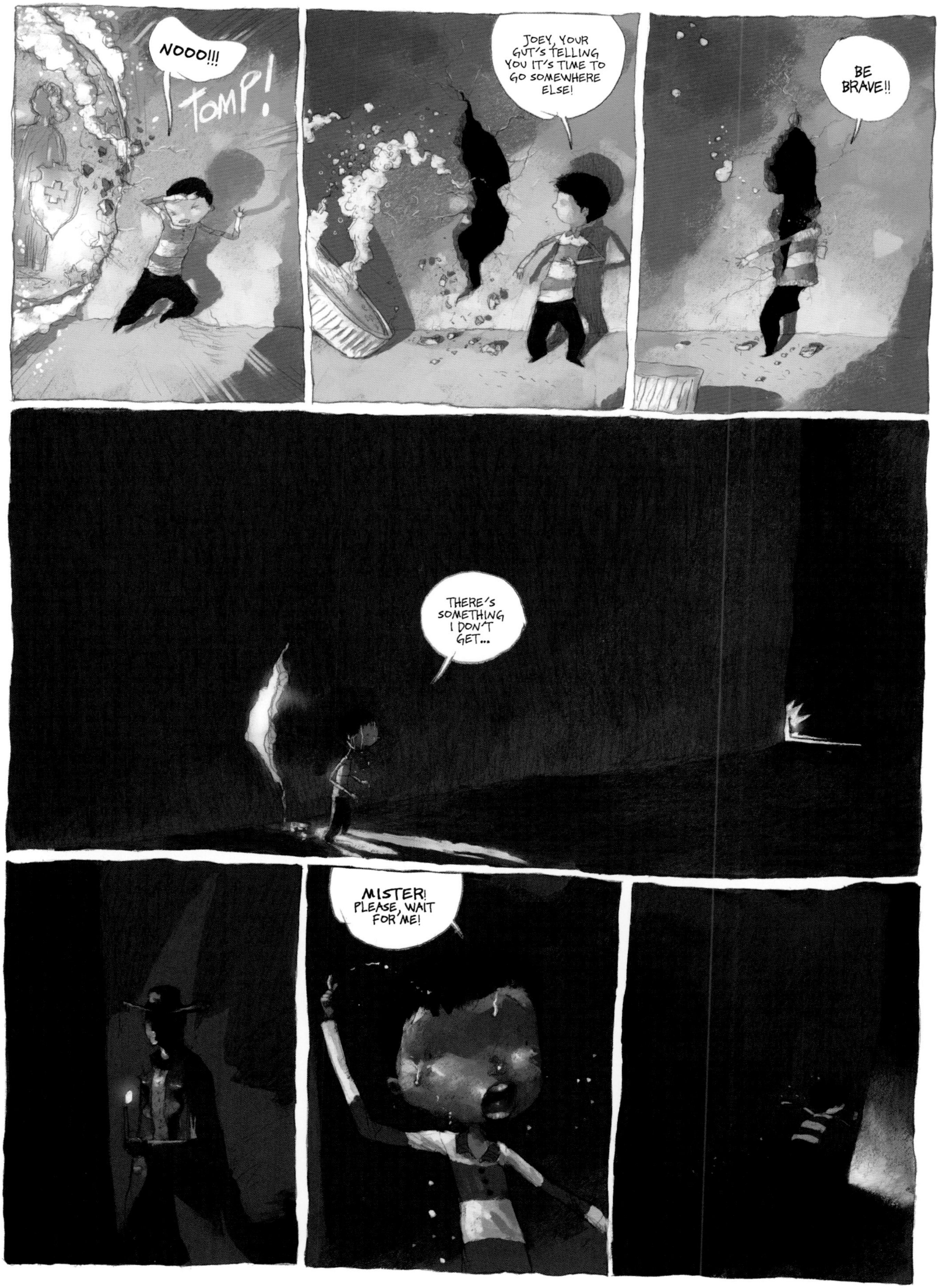
NOOO!!!
TOMP!
JOEY, YOUR GUT'S TELLING YOU IT'S TIME TO GO SOMEWHERE ELSE!
BE BRAVE!!
THERE'S SOMETHING I DON'T GET...
MISTER! PLEASE, WAIT FOR ME!

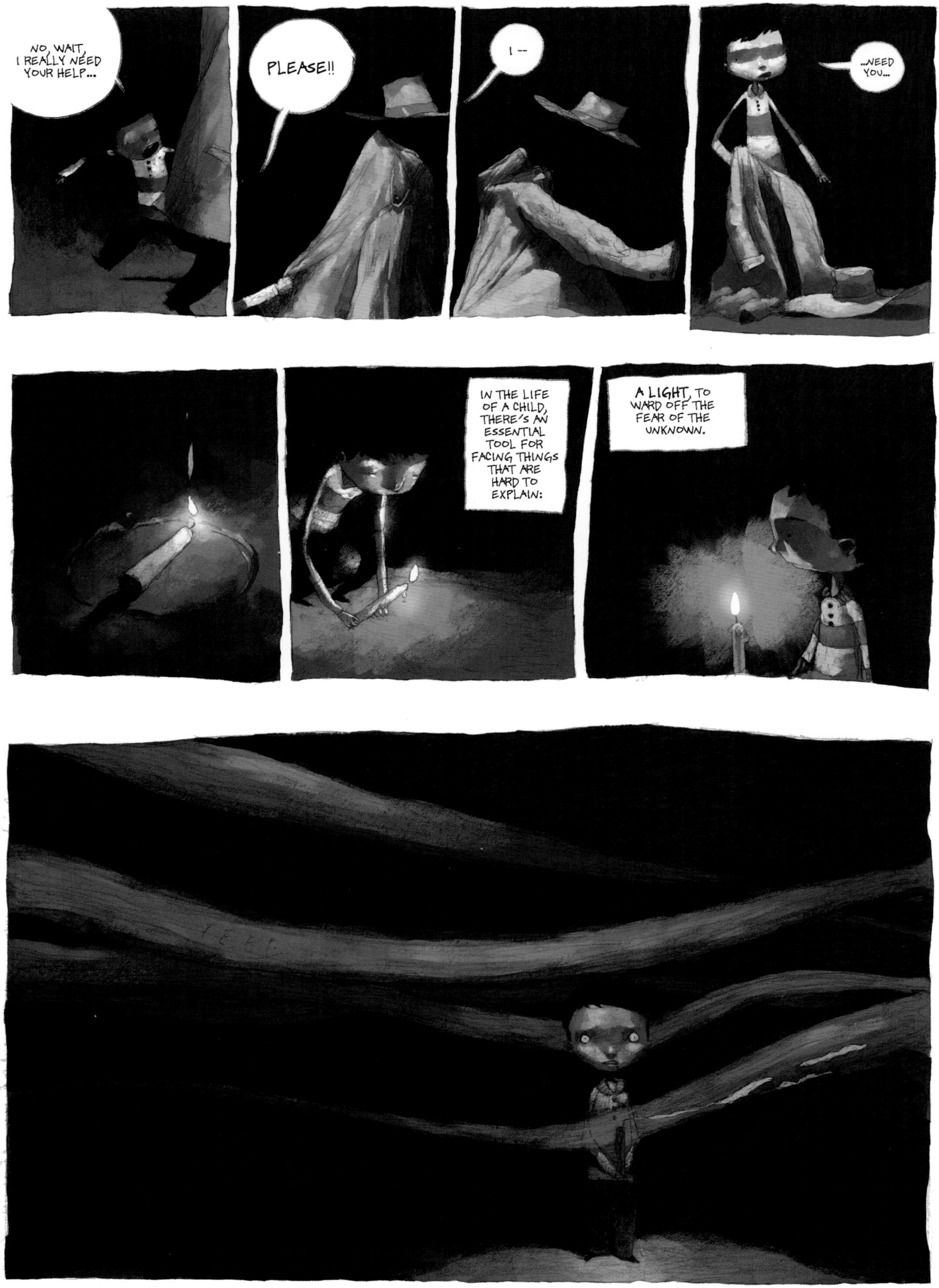
NO, WAIT, I REALLY NEED YOUR HELP...
PLEASE!!
I --
...NEED YOU...
IN THE LIFE OF A CHILD, THERE'S AN ESSENTIAL TOOL FOR FACING THINGS THAT ARE HARD TO EXPLAIN:
A LIGHT, TO WARD OFF THE FEAR OF THE UNKNOWN.

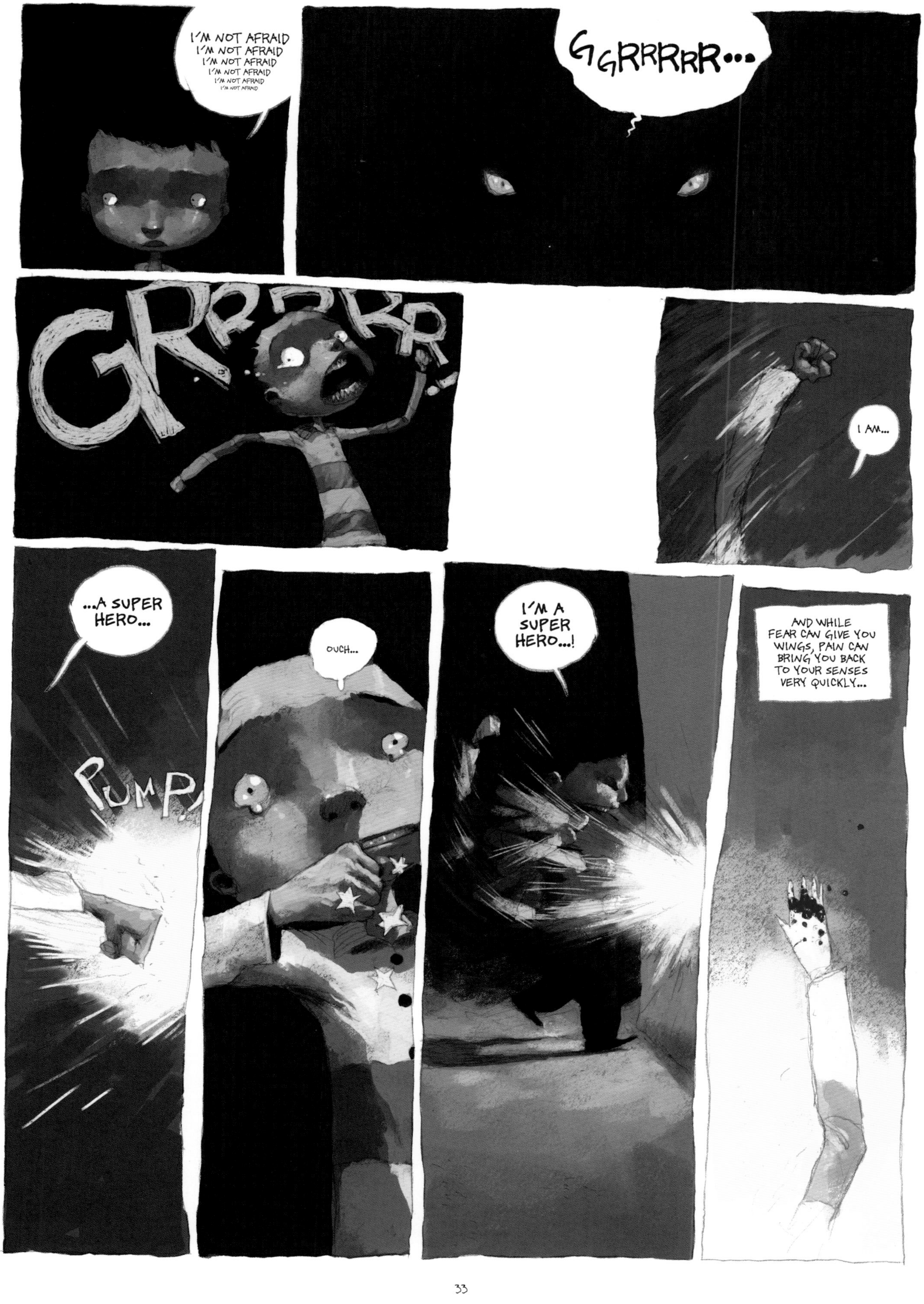
I'M NOT AFRAID I'M NOT AFRAID I'M NOT AFRAID I'M NOT AFRAID I'M NOT AFRAID I'M NOT AFRAID
GGRRRRRR...
GRRRRR
I AM...
...A SUPER HERO...
PUMP!
OUCH...
I'M A SUPER HERO...!
AND WHILE FEAR CAN GIVE YOU WINGS, PAIN CAN BRING YOU BACK TO YOUR SENSES VERY QUICKLY...

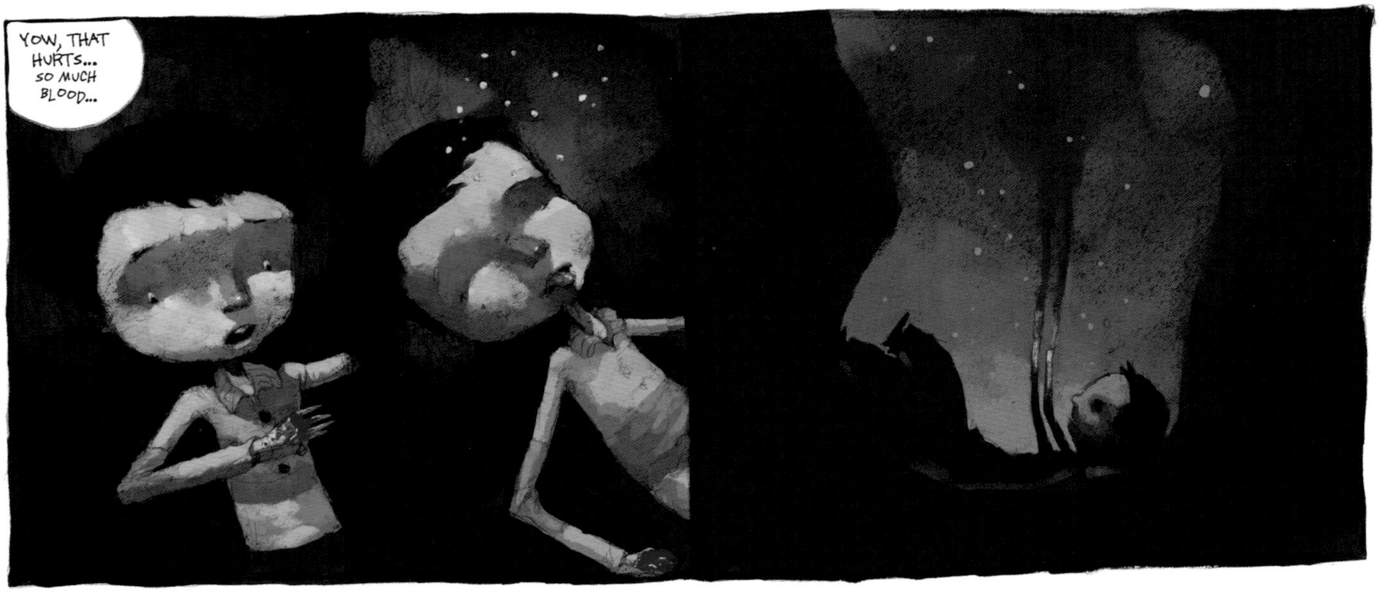
YOW, THAT HURTS... SO MUCH BLOOD...

FAINTING...
LEAVING MY PHYSICAL BODY.
FLOATING IN DARKNESS.
HOW CAN I DESCRIBE SUCH
A STATE OF BLISS?
IS THIS WHAT DEATH FEELS LIKE?

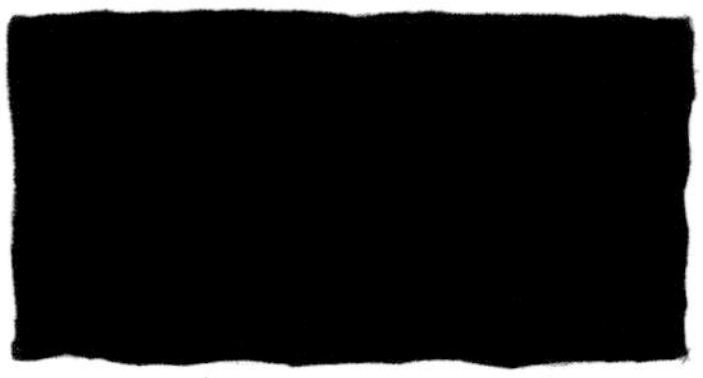

I WAS OKAY WITH IT.
I WASN'T AFRAID ANY MORE.
MY MIND FINALLY LET GO OF
THE OBSESSION TO RETURN
HOME.

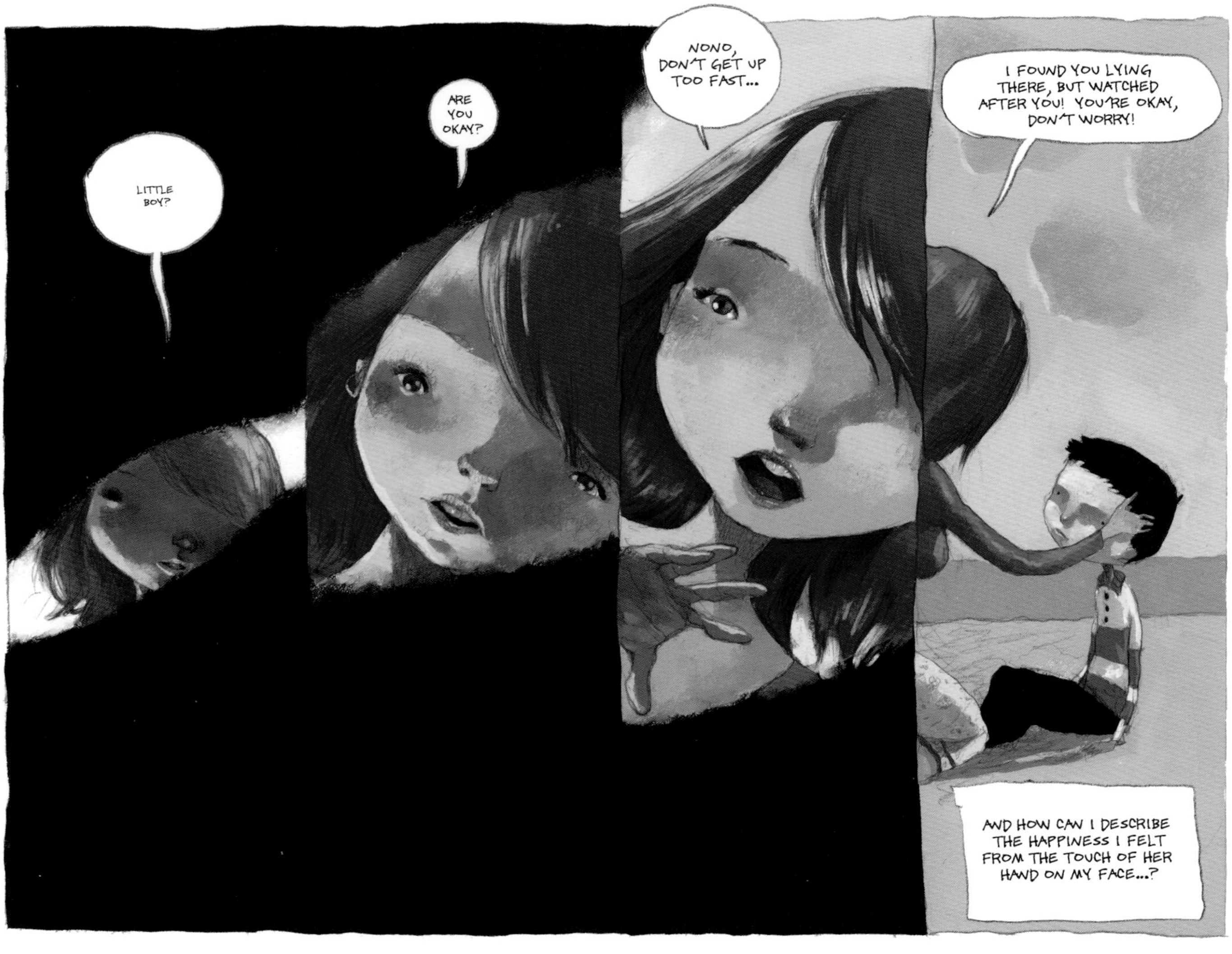
LITTLE BOY?
ARE YOU OKAY?
NONO, DON'T GET UP TOO FAST...
I FOUND YOU LYING THERE, BUT WATCHED AFTER YOU! YOU'RE OKAY, DON'T WORRY!
AND HOW CAN I DESCRIBE THE HAPPINESS I FELT FROM THE TOUCH OF HER HAND ON MY FACE...?

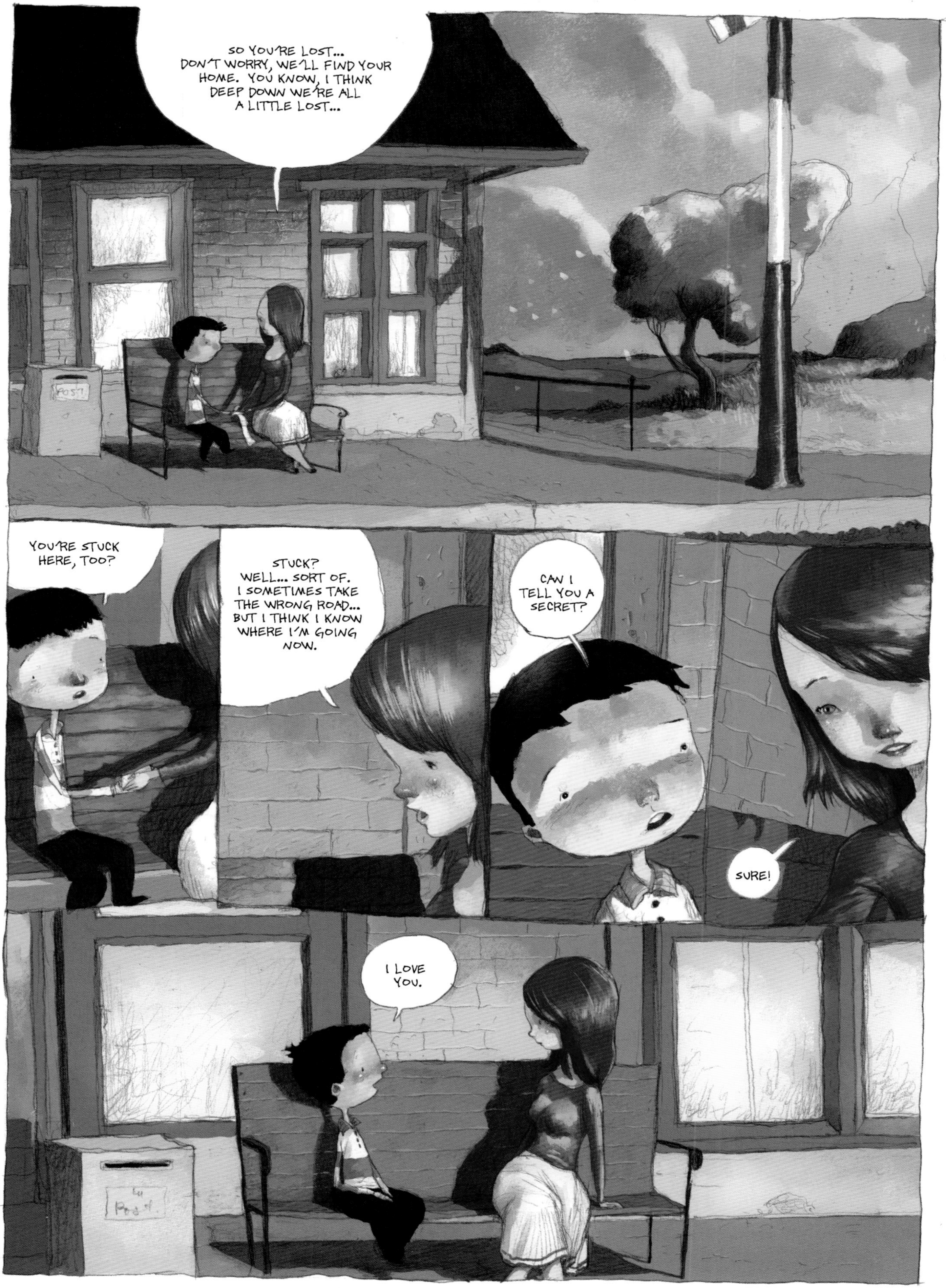
SO YOU'RE LOST... DON'T WORRY, WE'LL FIND YOUR HOME. YOU KNOW, I THINK DEEP DOWN WE'RE ALL A LITTLE LOST...
POST
YOU'RE STUCK HERE, TOO?
STUCK? WELL... SORT OF. I SOMETIMES TAKE THE WRONG ROAD... BUT I THINK I KNOW WHERE I'M GOING NOW.
CAN I TELL YOU A SECRET?
SURE!
I LOVE YOU.

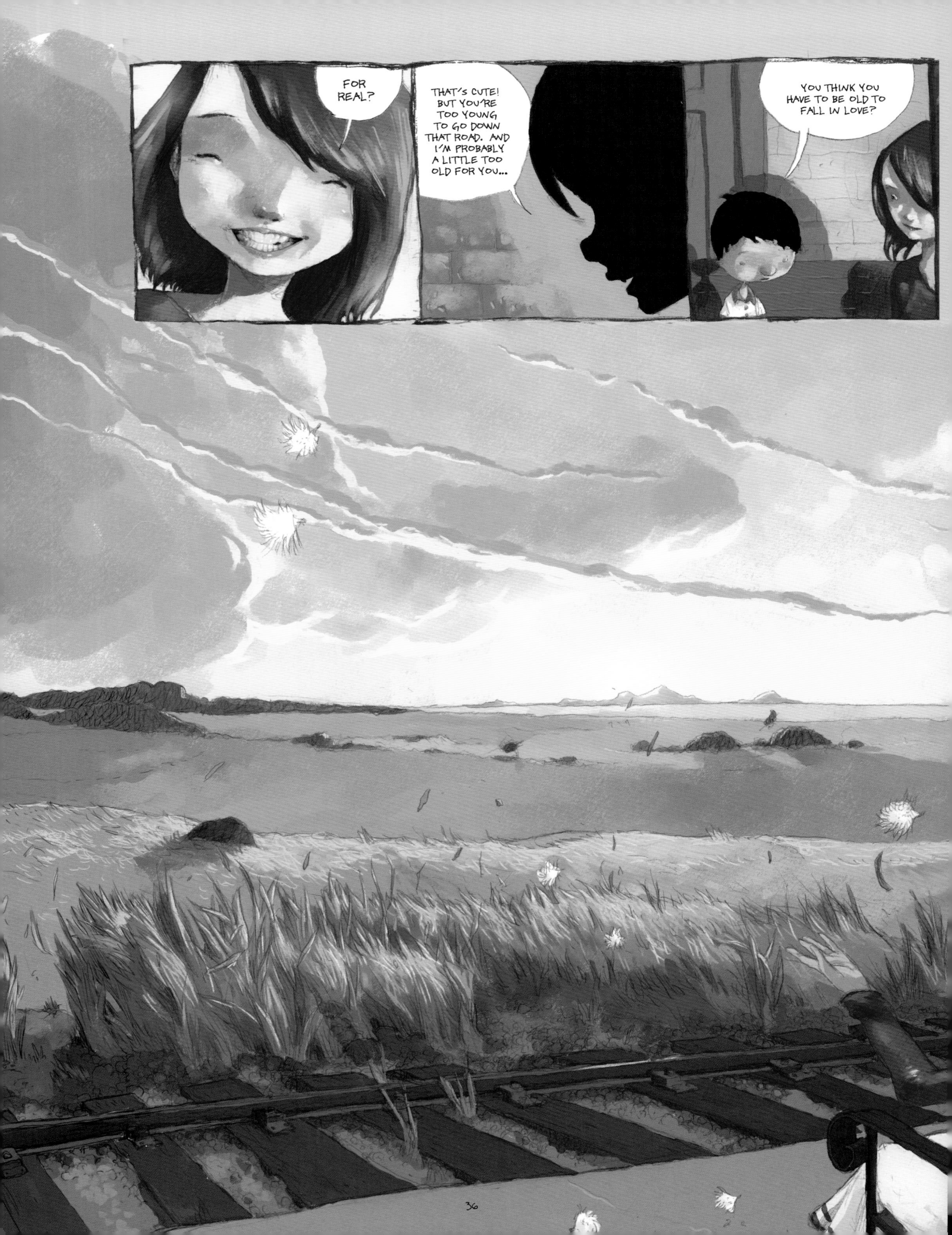
FOR REAL?
THAT'S CUTE! BUT YOU'RE TOO YOUNG TO GO DOWN THAT ROAD. AND I'M PROBABLY A LITTLE TOO OLD FOR YOU...
YOU THINK YOU HAVE TO BE OLD TO FALL IN LOVE?

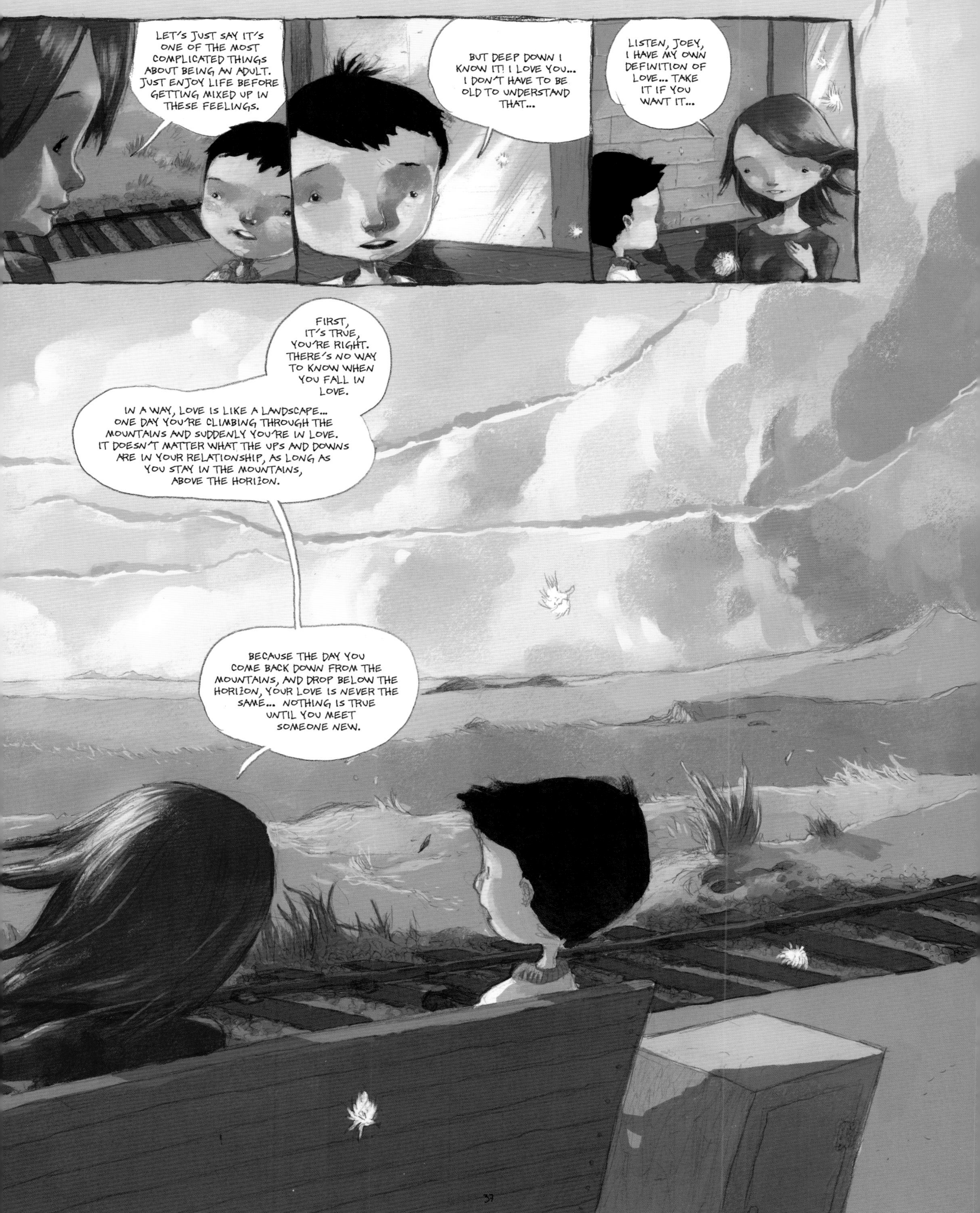

LET'S JUST SAY IT'S ONE OF THE MOST COMPLICATED THINGS ABOUT BEING AN ADULT. JUST ENJOY LIFE BEFORE GETTING MIXED UP IN THESE FEELINGS.
BUT DEEP DOWN I KNOW IT! I LOVE YOU... I DON'T HAVE TO BE OLD TO UNDERSTAND THAT...
LISTEN, JOEY, I HAVE MY OWN DEFINITION OF LOVE... TAKE IT IF YOU WANT IT...
FIRST, IT'S TRUE, YOU'RE RIGHT. THERE'S NO WAY TO KNOW WHEN YOU FALL IN LOVE.
IN A WAY, LOVE IS LIKE A LANDSCAPE... ONE DAY YOU'RE CLIMBING THROUGH THE MOUNTAINS AND SUDDENLY YOU'RE IN LOVE. IT DOESN'T MATTER WHAT THE UPS AND DOWNS ARE IN YOUR RELATIONSHIP, AS LONG AS YOU STAY IN THE MOUNTAINS, ABOVE THE HORIZON.
BECAUSE THE DAY YOU COME BACK DOWN FROM THE MOUNTAINS, AND DROP BELOW THE HORIZON, YOUR LOVE IS NEVER THE SAME... NOTHING IS TRUE UNTIL YOU MEET SOMEONE NEW.

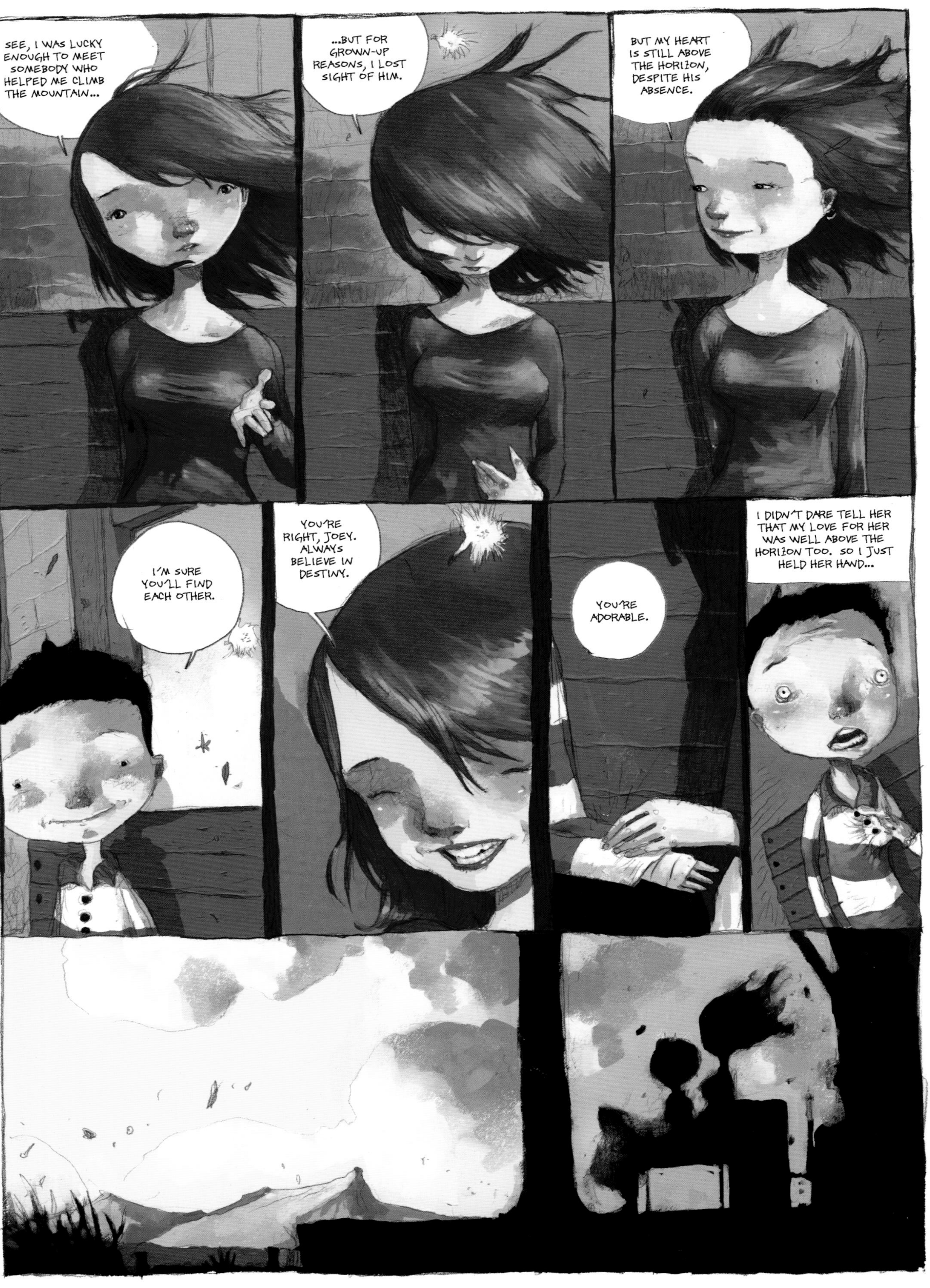
SEE, I WAS LUCKY ENOUGH TO MEET SOMEBODY WHO HELPED ME CLIMB THE MOUNTAIN...
...BUT FOR GROWN-UP REASONS, I LOST SIGHT OF HIM.
BUT MY HEART IS STILL ABOVE THE HORIZON, DESPITE HIS ABSENCE.
I'M SURE YOU'LL FIND EACH OTHER.
YOU'RE RIGHT, JOEY. ALWAYS BELIEVE IN DESTINY.
YOU'RE ADORABLE.
I DIDN'T DARE TELL HER THAT MY LOVE FOR HER WAS WELL ABOVE THE HORIZON TOO. SO I JUST HELD HER HAND...

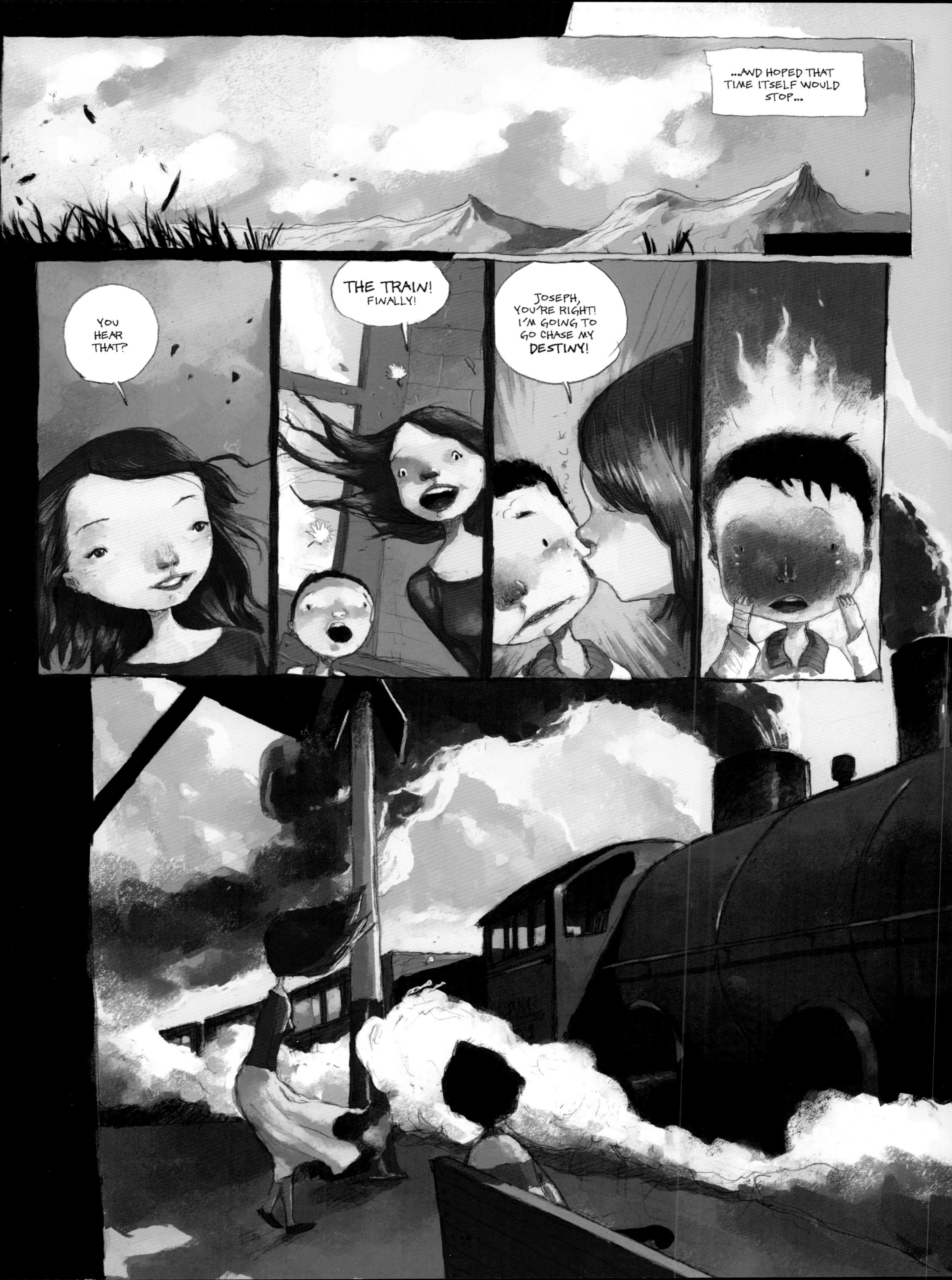
...AND HOPED THAT TIME ITSELF WOULD STOP...
YOU HEAR THAT?
THE TRAIN! FINALLY!
JOSEPH, YOU'RE RIGHT! I'M GOING TO GO CHASE MY DESTINY!

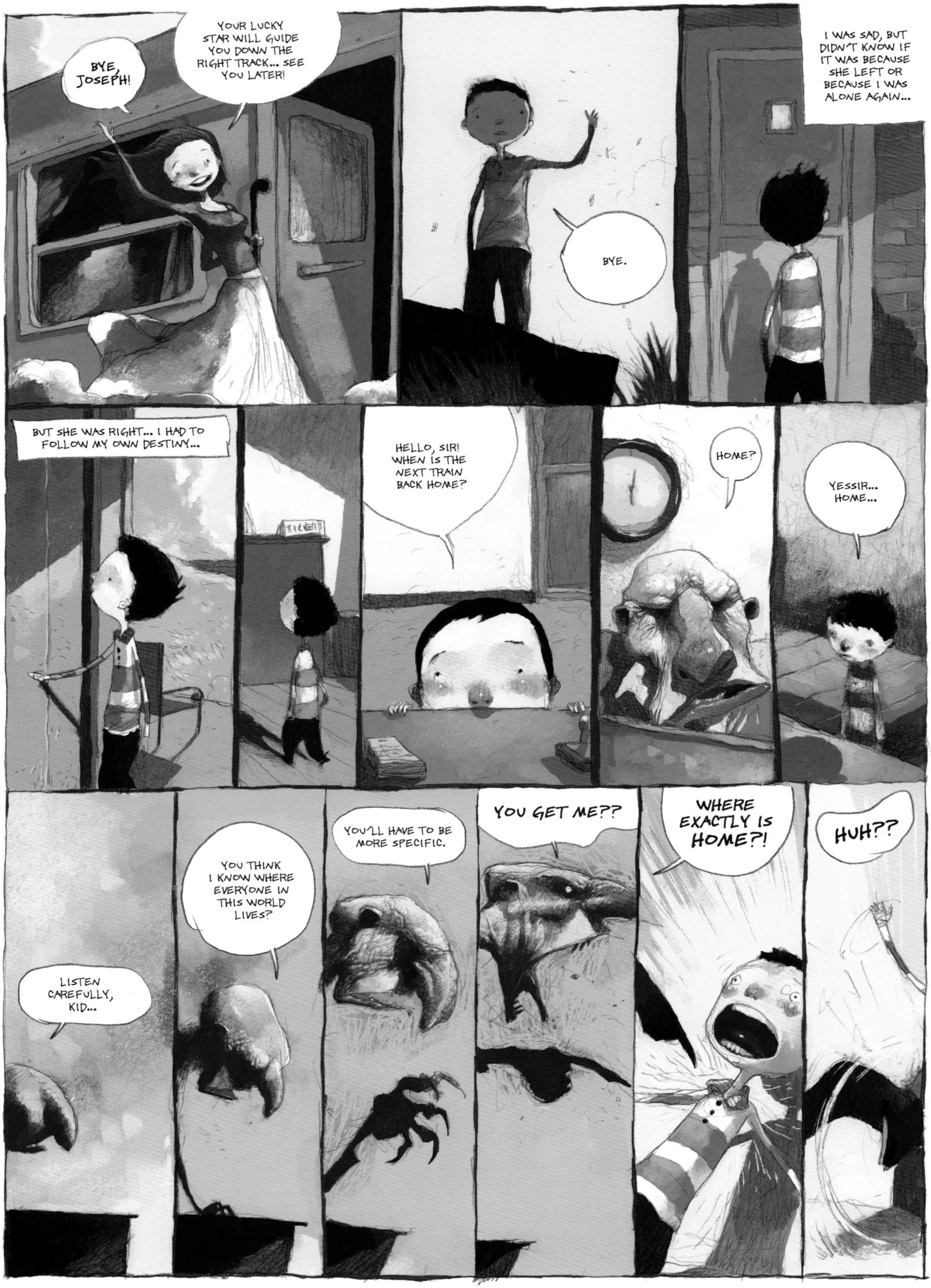
BYE, JOSEPH!
YOUR LUCKY STAR WILL GUIDE YOU DOWN THE RIGHT TRACK... SEE YOU LATER!
BYE.
I WAS SAD, BUT DIDN'T KNOW IF IT WAS BECAUSE SHE LEFT OR BECAUSE I WAS ALONE AGAIN...
BUT SHE WAS RIGHT... I HAD TO FOLLOW MY OWN DESTINY...
TICKETS
HELLO, SIR! WHEN IS THE NEXT TRAIN BACK HOME?
HOME?
YESSIR... HOME...
LISTEN CAREFULLY, KID...
YOU THINK I KNOW WHERE EVERYONE IN THIS WORLD LIVES?
YOU'LL HAVE TO BE MORE SPECIFIC.
YOU GET ME??
WHERE EXACTLY IS HOME?!
HUH??

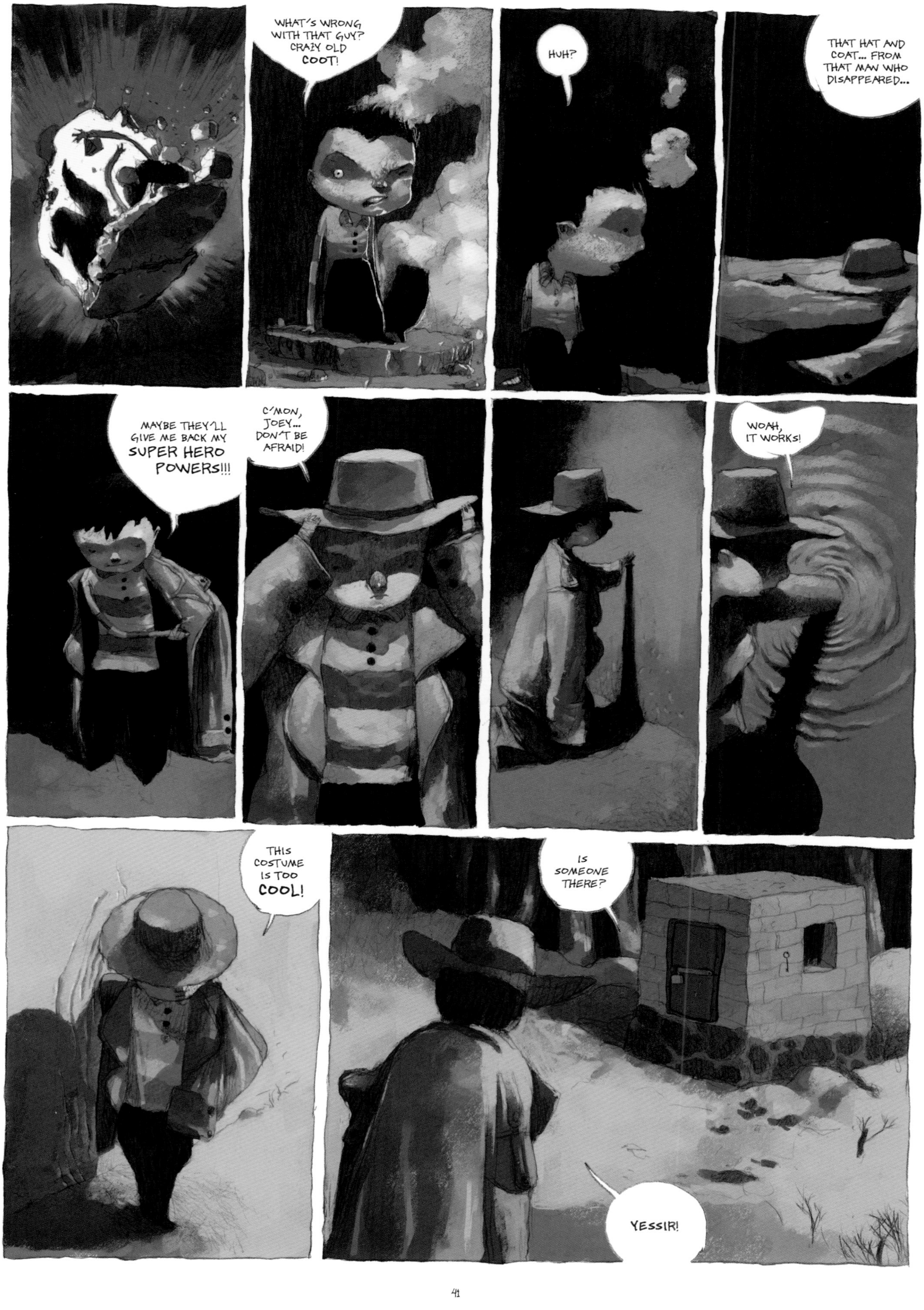

WHAT'S WRONG WITH THAT GUY? CRAZY OLD COOT!
HUH?
THAT HAT AND COAT... FROM THAT MAN WHO DISAPPEARED...
MAYBE THEY'LL GIVE ME BACK MY SUPER HERO POWERS!!!
C'MON, JOEY... DON'T BE AFRAID!
WOAH, IT WORKS!
THIS COSTUME IS TOO COOL!
IS SOMEONE THERE?
YESSIR!

WHAT'S YOUR NAME?

JOSEPH.

HOW OLD ARE YOU?

ELEVEN.

WHAT ARE YOU DOING OUT HERE?

I'M LOST.

DO YOU WANT ME TO HELP YOU?

YESSIR.

GOOD, ME TOO. SEE, KID, I WAS LOST ONCE...

...SO I BUILT THIS PRISON TO PROTECT ME, AS PUNISHMENT FOR MY OWN STUPID MISTAKES... SO I COULD BATTLE MY OWN DEMONS...

...BUT I'M ALL BETTER NOW, SEE...?

AND YOU, JOSEPH, YOU'LL BE THE ANGEL WHO WILL SET ME FREE...

BUT YOU HAVE TO PROMISE THIS'LL BE OUR LITTLE SECRET, JUST BETWEEN US. GOT IT?

SURE, I PROMISE, MISTER.

YOU SEE THE KEY THERE NEXT TO THE WINDOW?

YEAH.

TAKE IT AND OPEN THE DOOR.

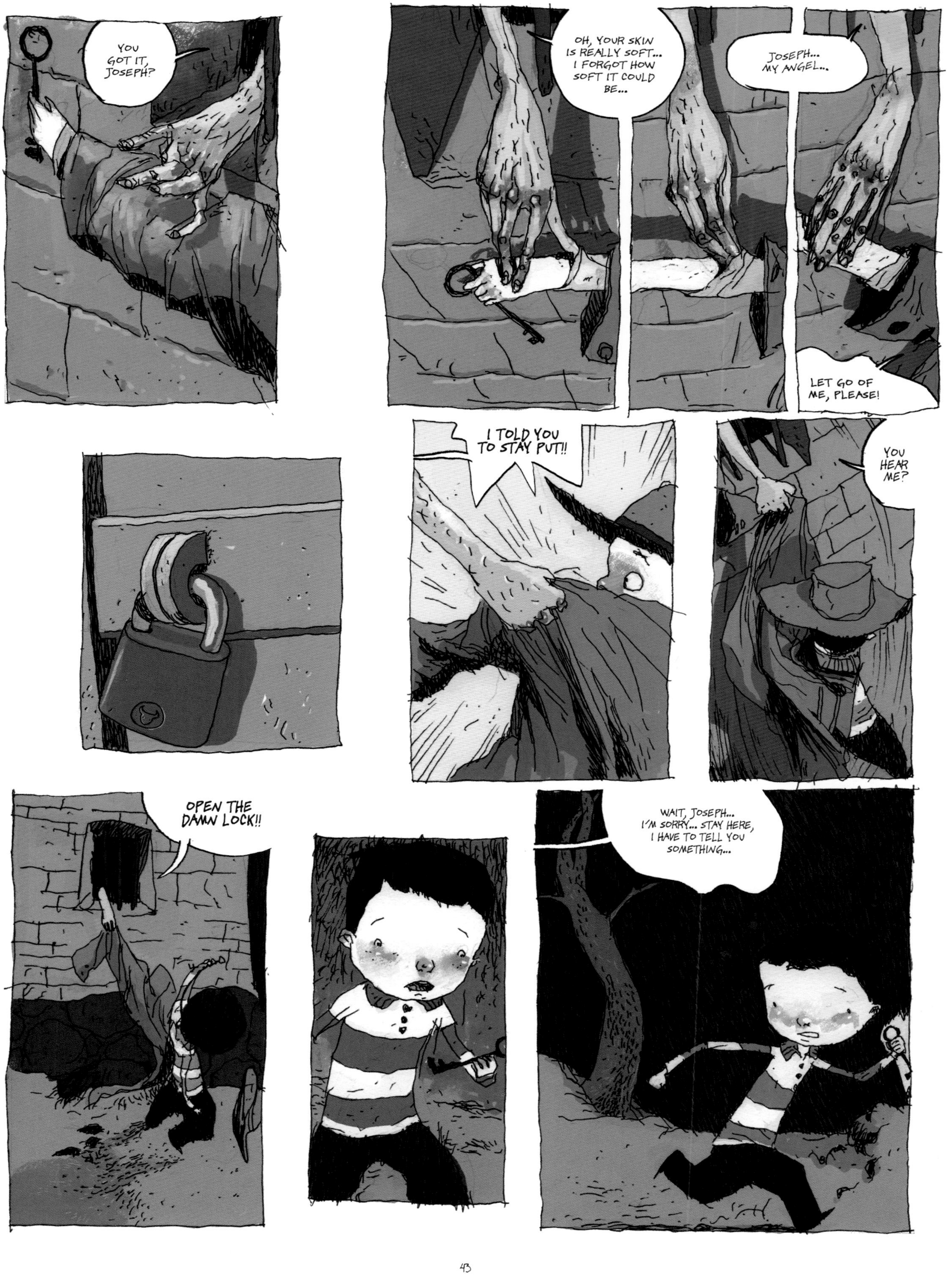
YOU GOT IT, JOSEPH?
OH, YOUR SKIN IS REALLY SOFT... I FORGOT HOW SOFT IT COULD BE...
JOSEPH... MY ANGEL...
LET GO OF ME, PLEASE!
I TOLD YOU TO STAY PUT!!
YOU HEAR ME?
OPEN THE DAMN LOCK!!
WAIT, JOSEPH... I'M SORRY... STAY HERE, I HAVE TO TELL YOU SOMETHING...

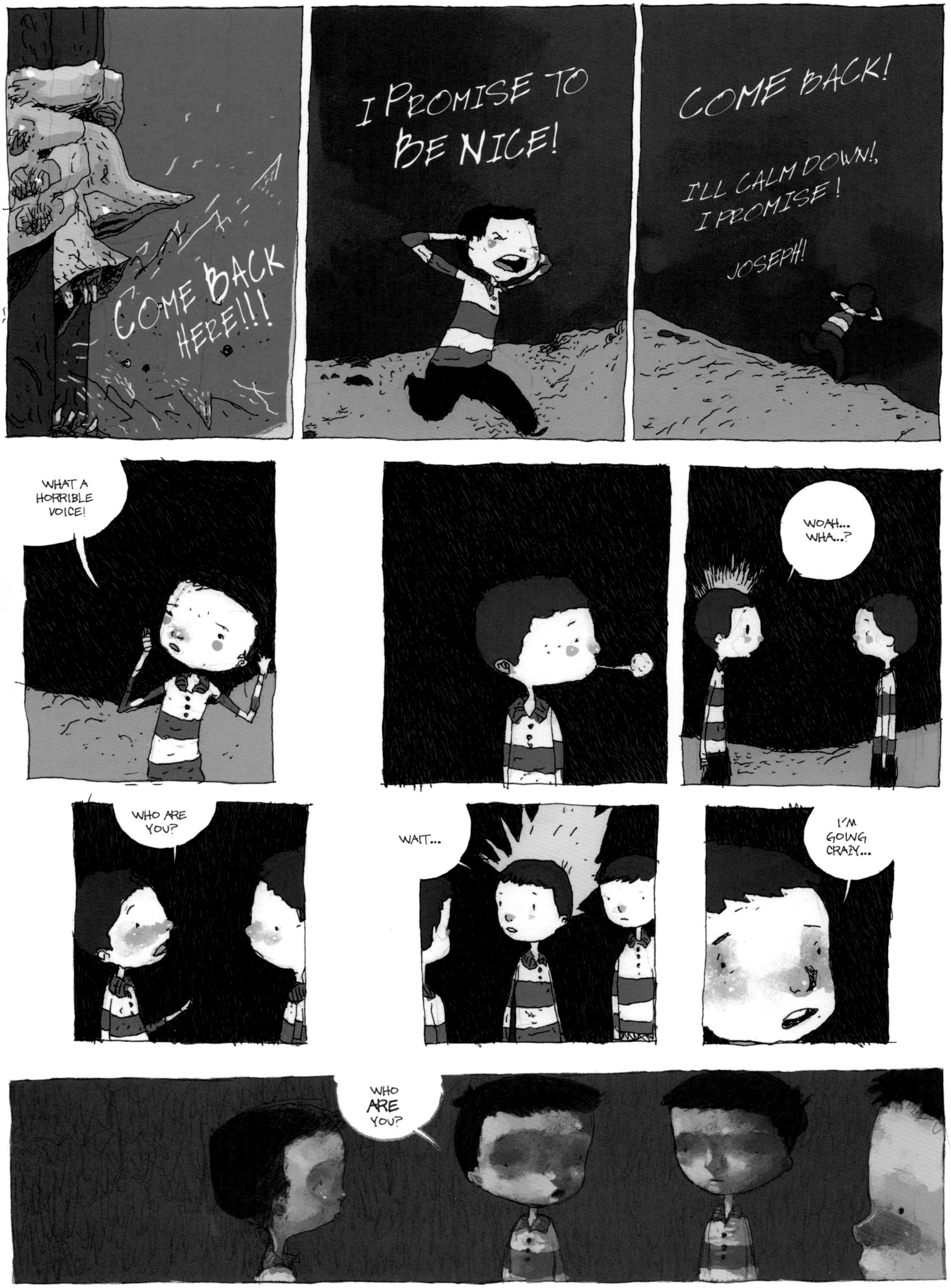
COME BACK HERE!!!
I PROMISE TO BE NICE!
COME BACK!
I'LL CALM DOWN!, I PROMISE!
JOSEPH!
WHAT A HORRIBLE VOICE!
WOAH... WHA...?
WHO ARE YOU?
WAIT...
I'M GOING CRAZY...
WHO ARE YOU?

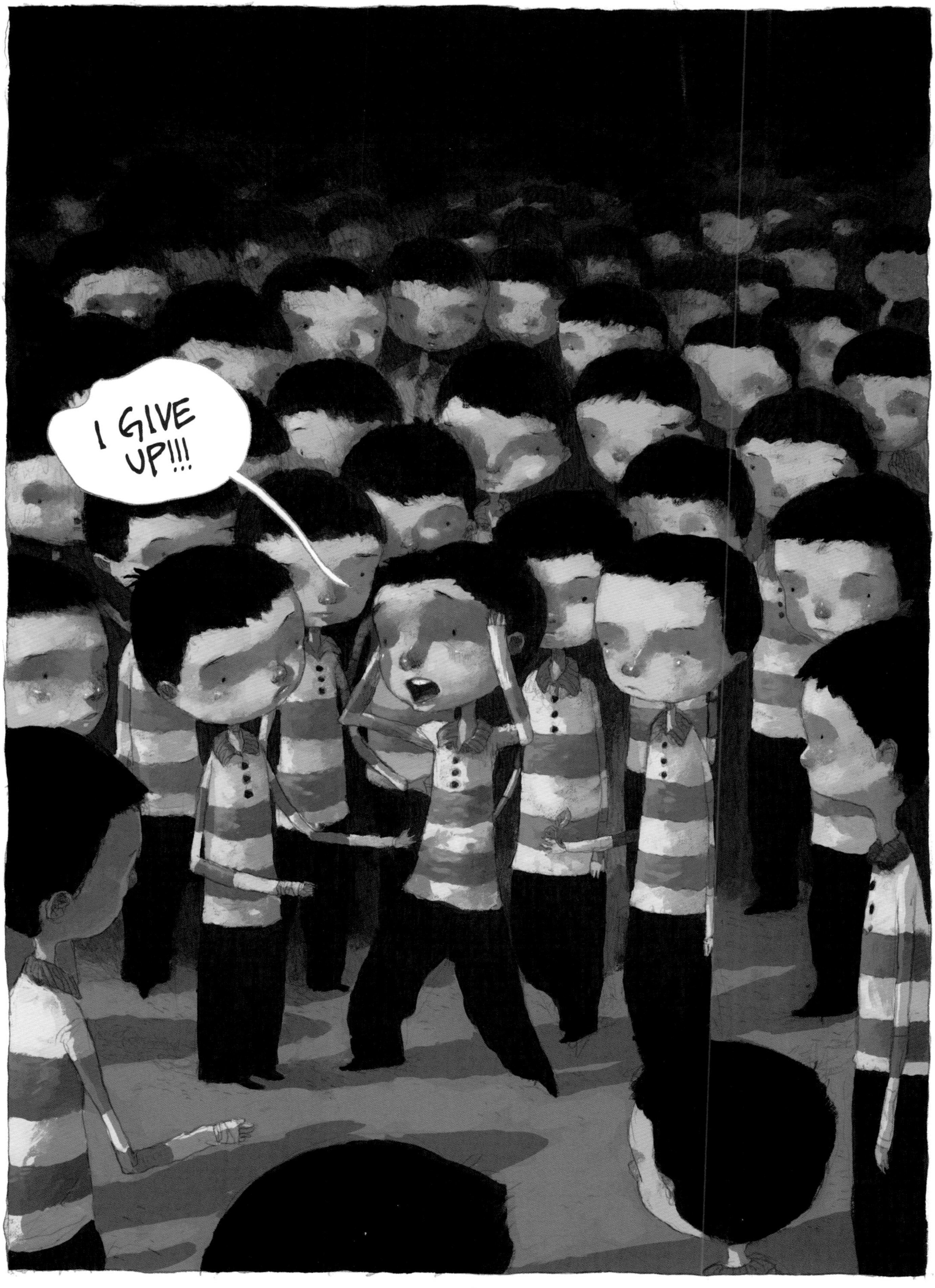
I GIVE UP!!!

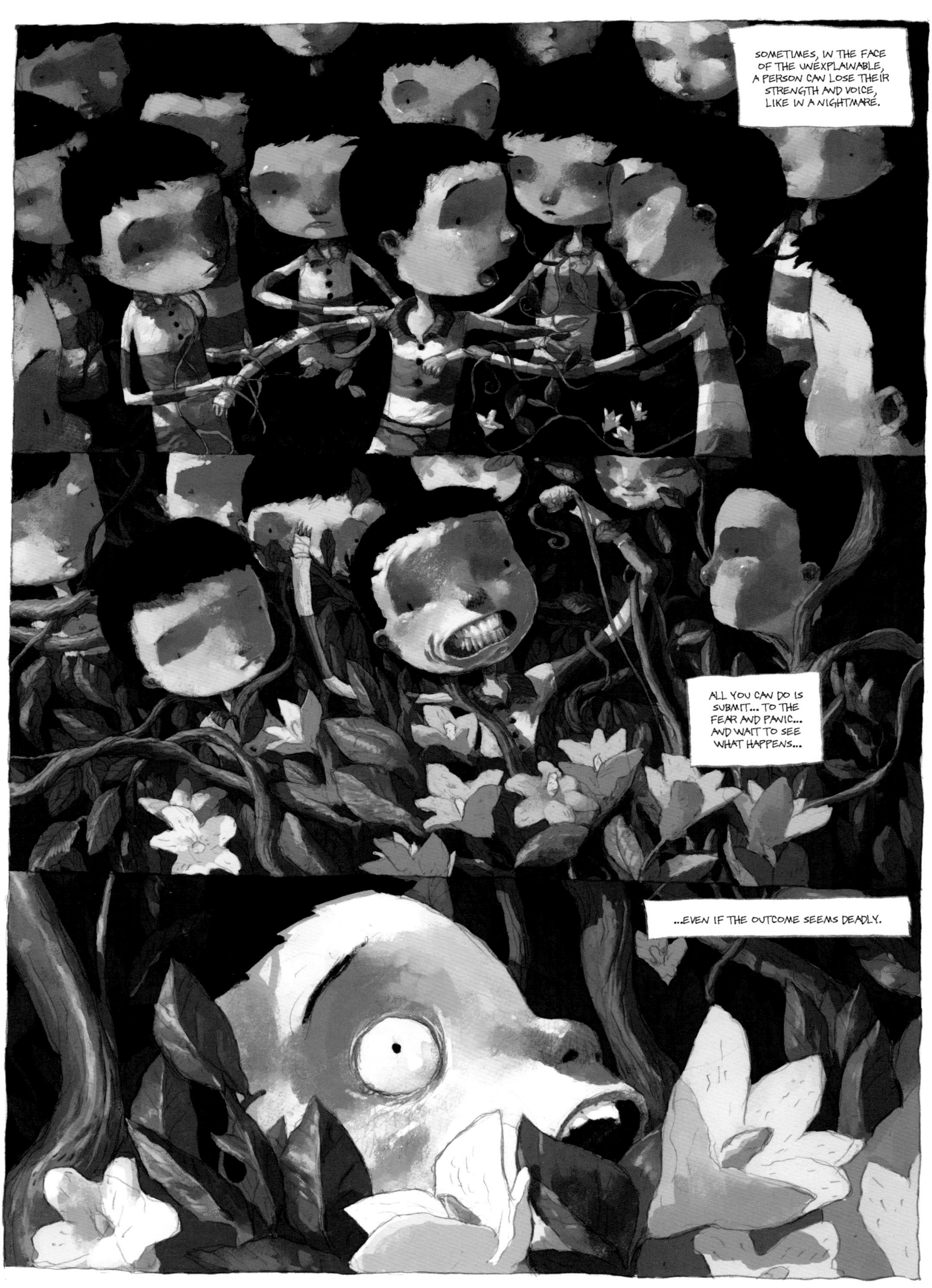
SOMETIMES, IN THE FACE OF THE UNEXPLAINABLE, A PERSON CAN LOSE THEIR STRENGTH AND VOICE, LIKE IN A NIGHTMARE.
ALL YOU CAN DO IS SUBMIT... TO THE FEAR AND PANIC... AND WAIT TO SEE WHAT HAPPENS...
...EVEN IF THE OUTCOME SEEMS DEADLY.

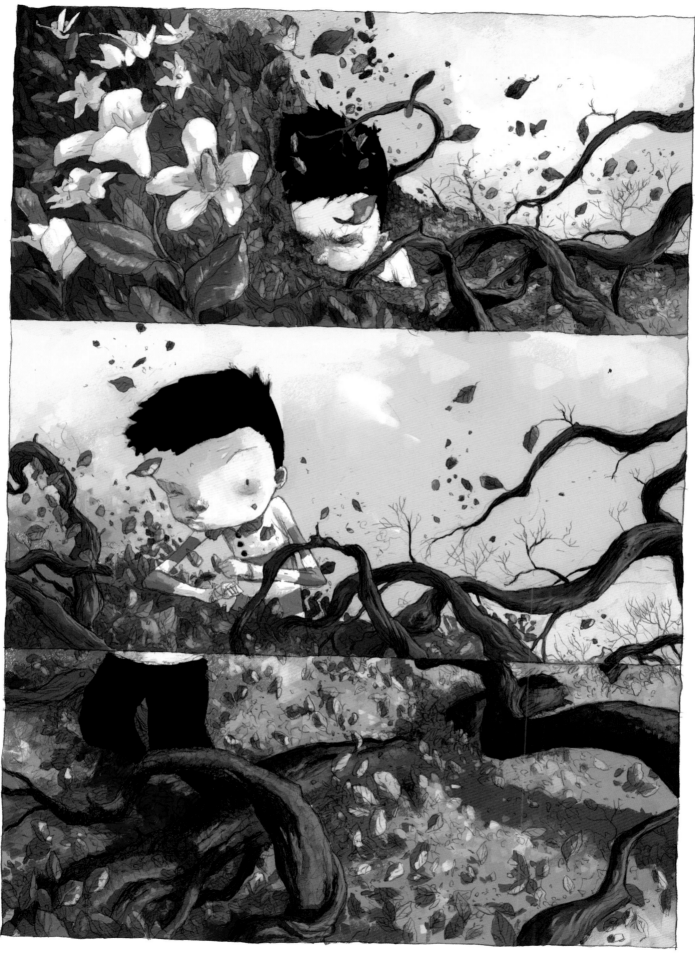

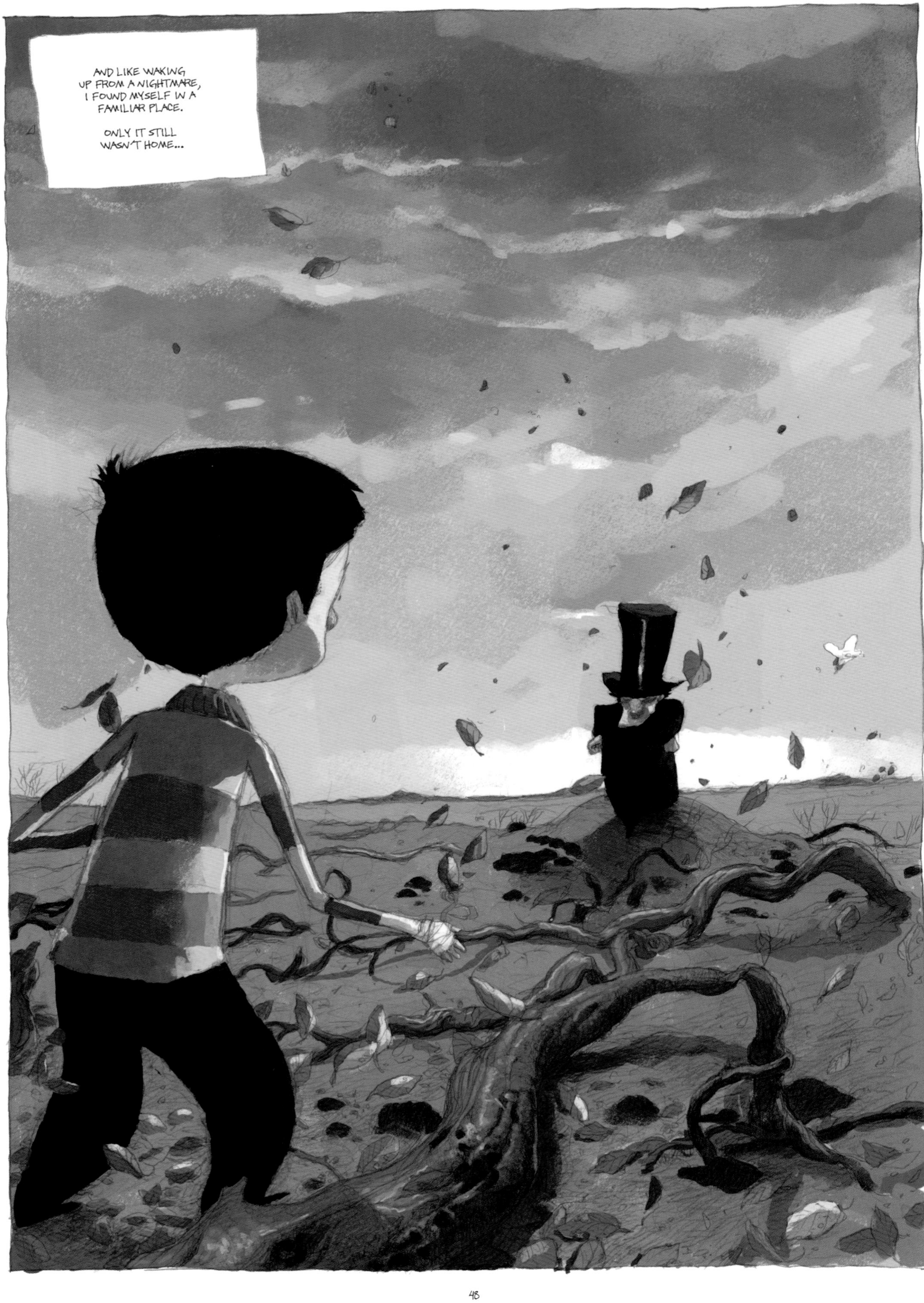
AND LIKE WAKING UP FROM A NIGHTMARE, I FOUND MYSELF IN A FAMILIAR PLACE.
ONLY IT STILL WASN'T HOME...

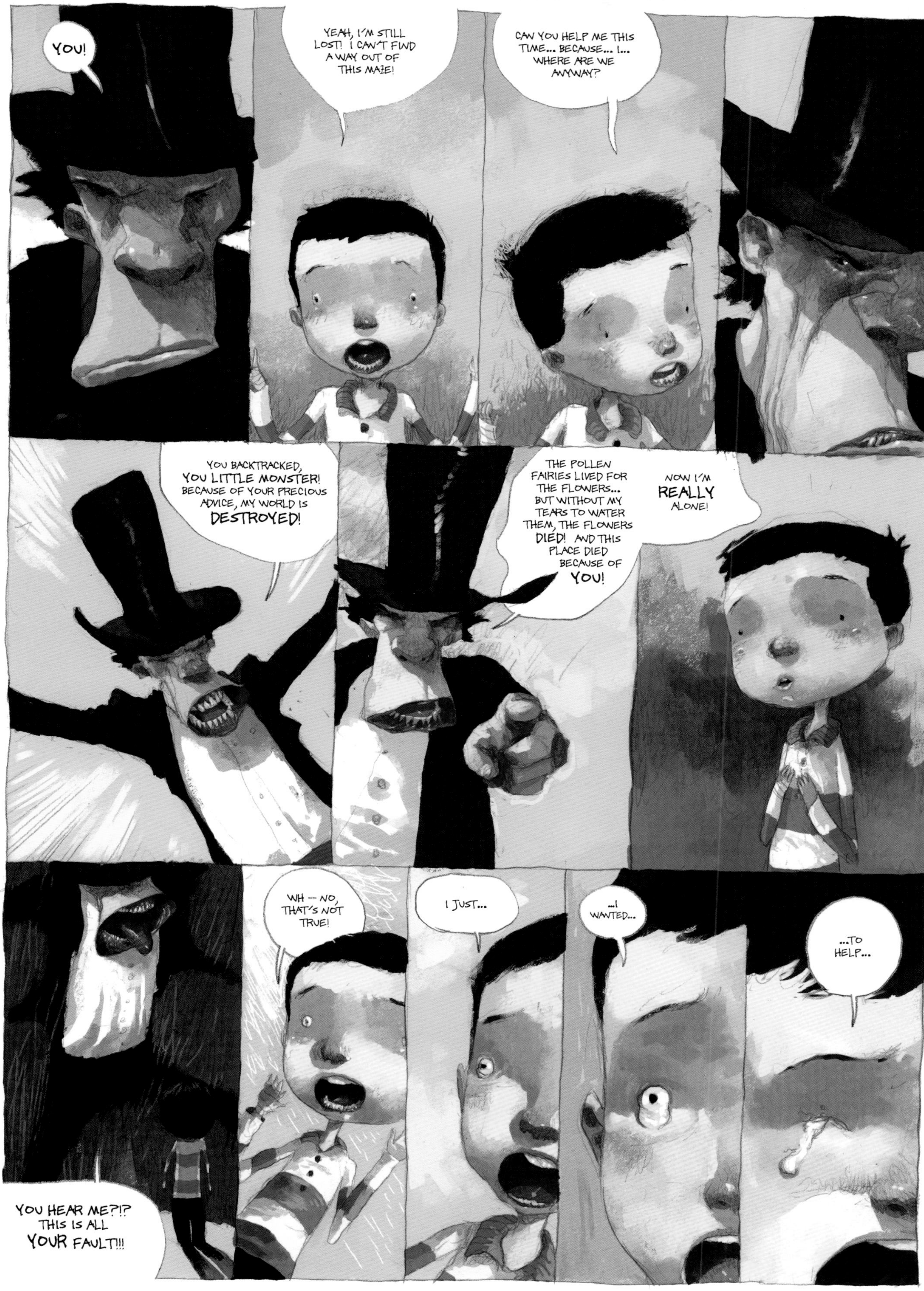
YOU!
YEAH, I'M STILL LOST! I CAN'T FIND A WAY OUT OF THIS MAZE!
CAN YOU HELP ME THIS TIME... BECAUSE... I... WHERE ARE WE ANYWAY?
YOU BACKTRACKED, YOU LITTLE MONSTER! BECAUSE OF YOUR PRECIOUS ADVICE, MY WORLD IS DESTROYED!
THE POLLEN FAIRIES LIVED FOR THE FLOWERS... BUT WITHOUT MY TEARS TO WATER THEM, THE FLOWERS DIED! AND THIS PLACE DIED BECAUSE OF YOU!
NOW I'M REALLY ALONE!
YOU HEAR ME?!? THIS IS ALL YOUR FAULT!!!
WH — NO, THAT'S NOT TRUE!
I JUST...
...I WANTED...
...TO HELP...

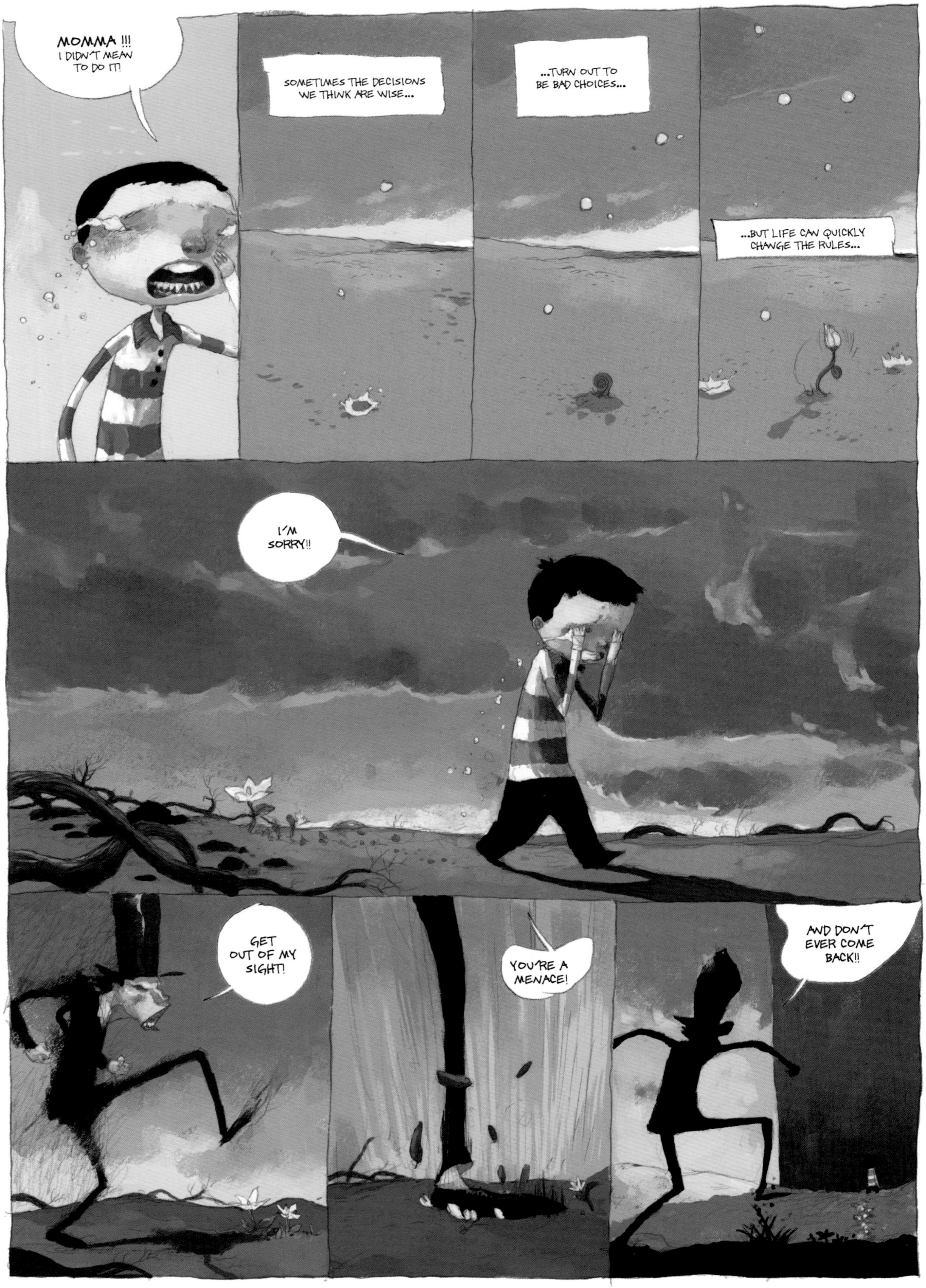
MOMMA !!! I DIDN'T MEAN TO DO IT!
SOMETIMES THE DECISIONS WE THINK ARE WISE...
...TURN OUT TO BE BAD CHOICES...
...BUT LIFE CAN QUICKLY CHANGE THE RULES...
I'M SORRY!!
GET OUT OF MY SIGHT!
YOU'RE A MENACE!
AND DON'T EVER COME BACK!!

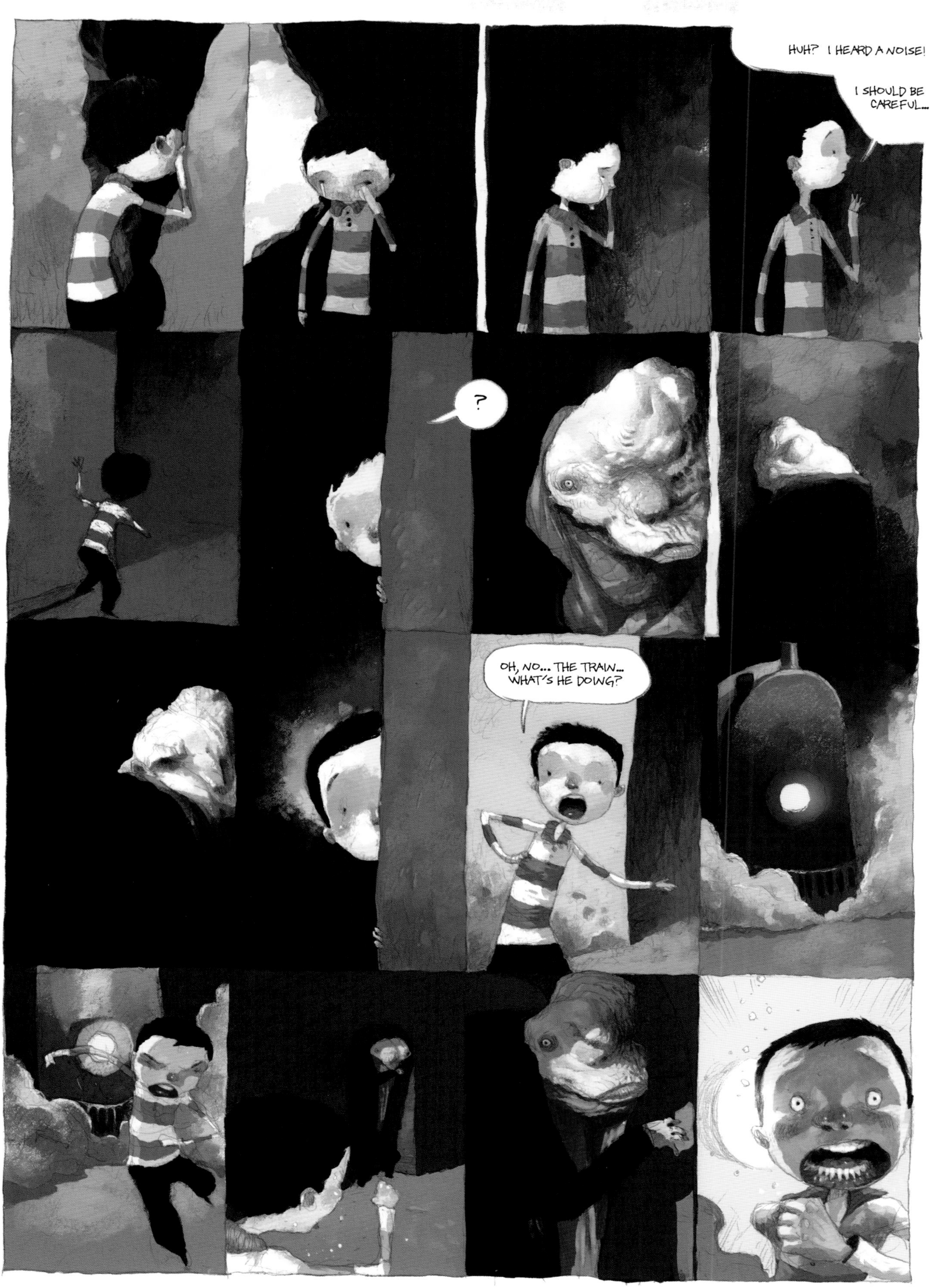
HUH? I HEARD A NOISE!
I SHOULD BE CAREFUL...
?
OH, NO... THE TRAIN... WHAT'S HE DOING?

FASTERRRR!!!

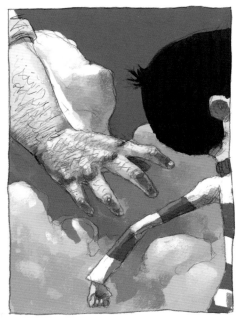

C'MERE, LITTLE GUY...

FUNNY GAME FOR YOUR AGE, JUNIOR!

BUT I WASN'T PLAYING...

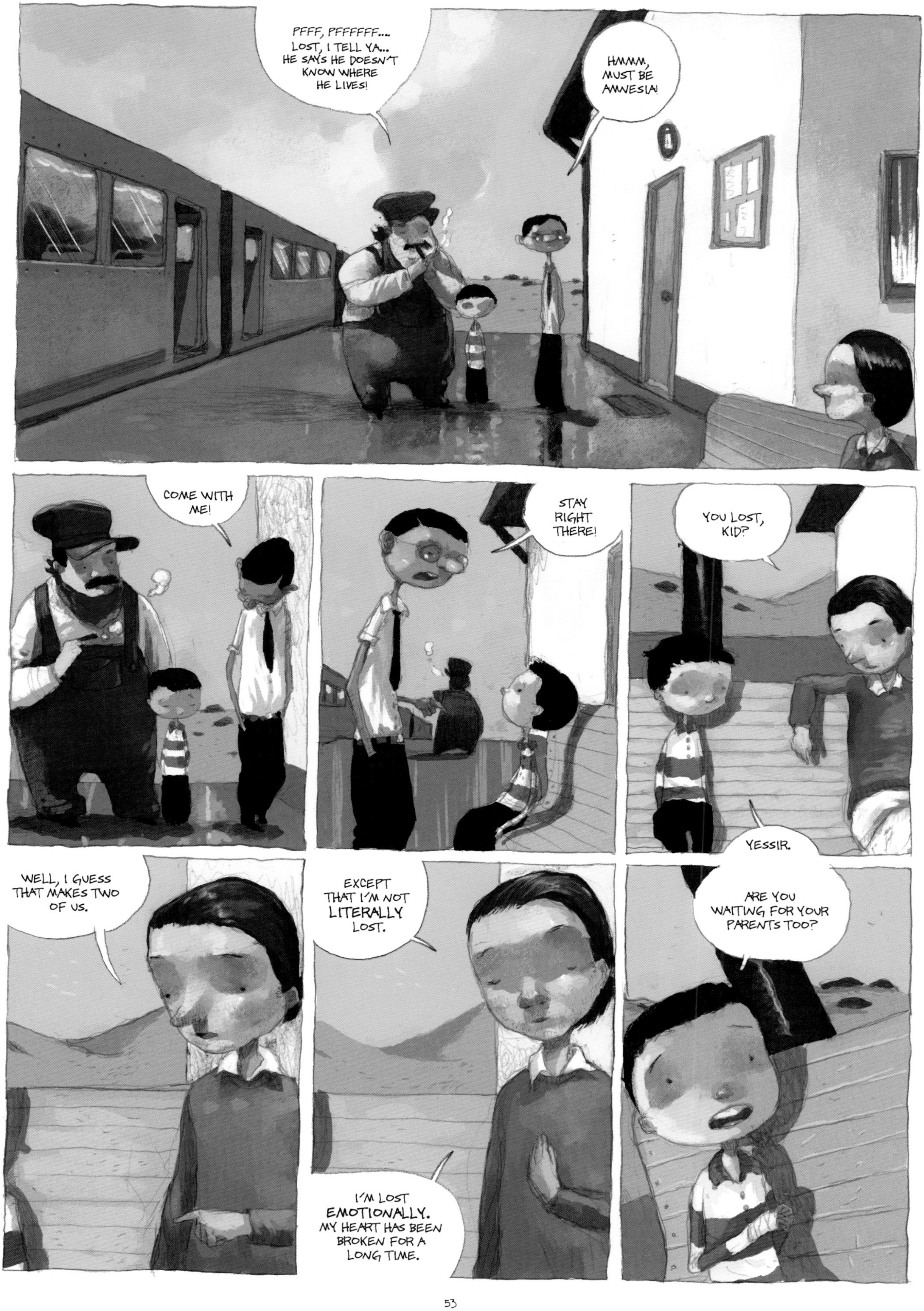

PFFF, PFFFFFF... LOST, I TELL YA... HE SAYS HE DOESN'T KNOW WHERE HE LIVES!
HMMM, MUST BE AMNESIA!
COME WITH ME!
STAY RIGHT THERE!
YOU LOST, KID?
YESSIR.
WELL, I GUESS THAT MAKES TWO OF US.
EXCEPT THAT I'M NOT LITERALLY LOST.
I'M LOST EMOTIONALLY. MY HEART HAS BEEN BROKEN FOR A LONG TIME.
ARE YOU WAITING FOR YOUR PARENTS TOO?

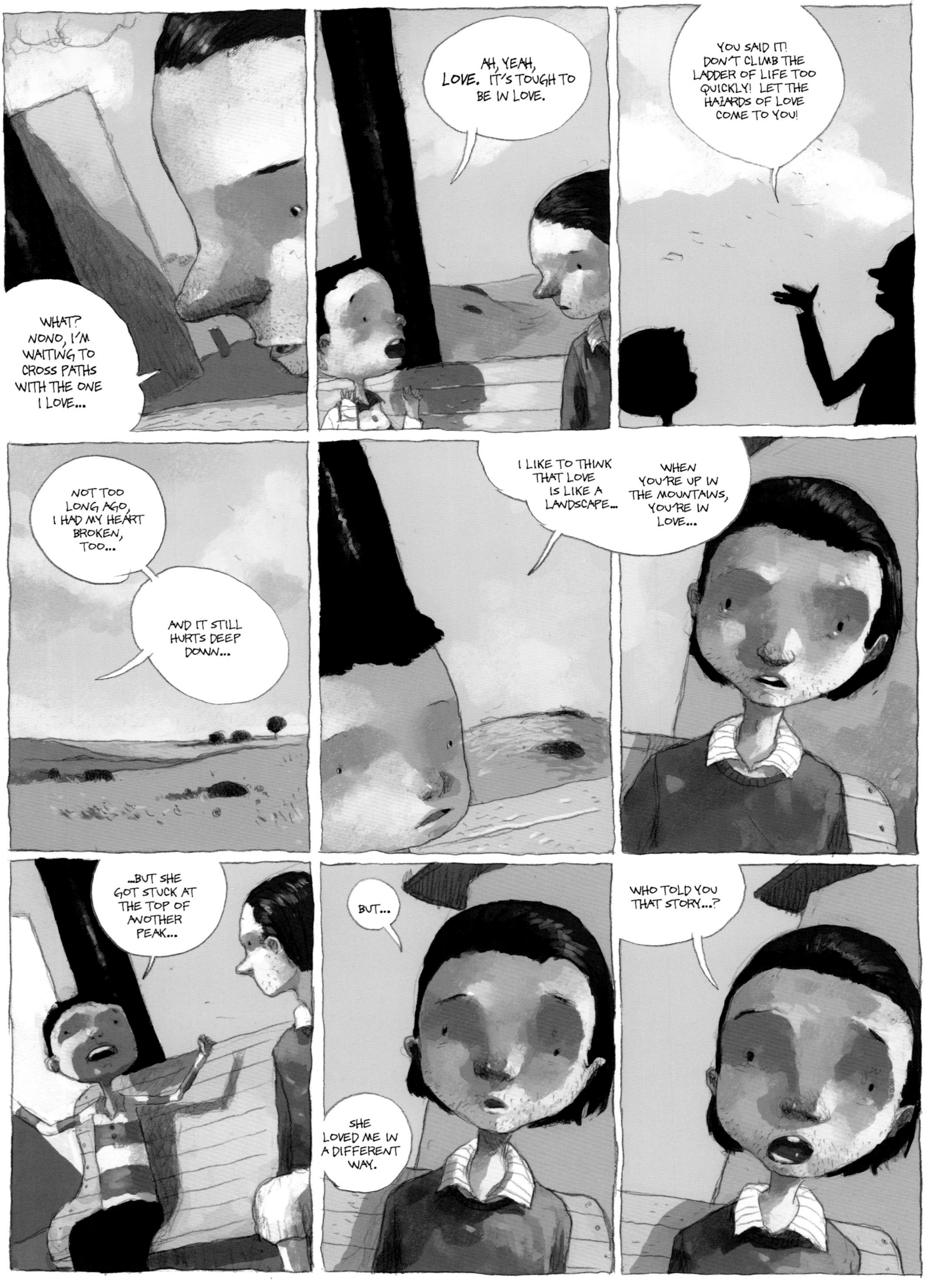
WHAT? NONO, I'M WAITING TO CROSS PATHS WITH THE ONE I LOVE...
AH, YEAH, LOVE. IT'S TOUGH TO BE IN LOVE.
YOU SAID IT! DON'T CLIMB THE LADDER OF LIFE TOO QUICKLY! LET THE HAZARDS OF LOVE COME TO YOU!
NOT TOO LONG AGO, I HAD MY HEART BROKEN, TOO...
AND IT STILL HURTS DEEP DOWN...
I LIKE TO THINK THAT LOVE IS LIKE A LANDSCAPE...
WHEN YOU'RE UP IN THE MOUNTAINS, YOU'RE IN LOVE...
...BUT SHE GOT STUCK AT THE TOP OF ANOTHER PEAK...
BUT...
SHE LOVED ME IN A DIFFERENT WAY.
WHO TOLD YOU THAT STORY...?

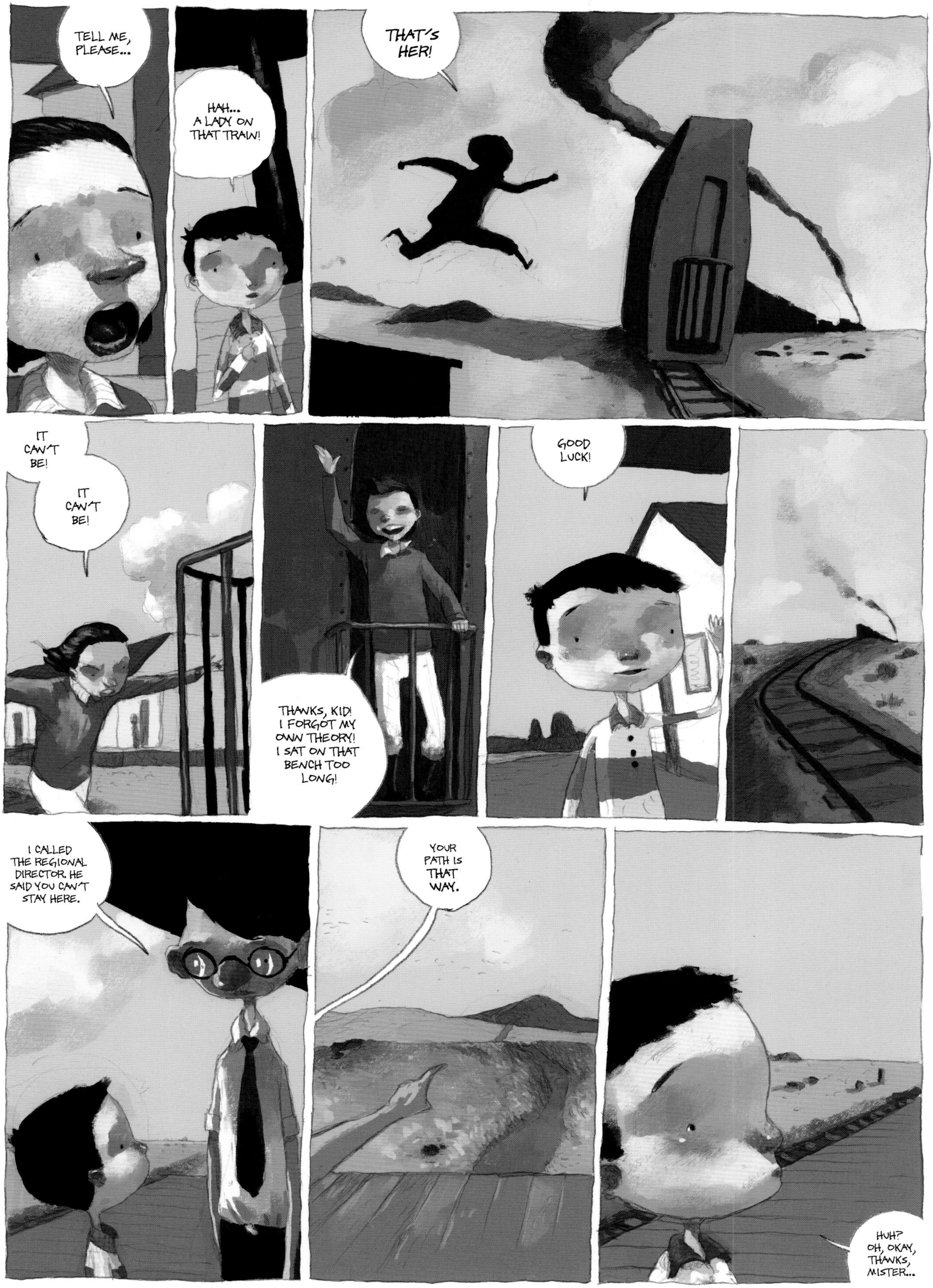

TELL ME, PLEASE...
HAH... A LADY ON THAT TRAIN!
THAT'S HER!
IT CAN'T BE!
IT CAN'T BE!
THANKS, KID! I FORGOT MY OWN THEORY! I SAT ON THAT BENCH TOO LONG!
GOOD LUCK!
I CALLED THE REGIONAL DIRECTOR. HE SAID YOU CAN'T STAY HERE.
YOUR PATH IS THAT WAY.
HUH? OH, OKAY, THANKS, MISTER...

MY PATH...

WHAT PATH?

SOMETIMES, WHEN YOU'RE JUST WANDERING, A WELL-WORN TRAIL CAN BE SAFER THAN FOLLOWING SOME LUCKY STAR...

HE SAID A PATH! WHAT'D HE THINK? THAT I CAN FLY?

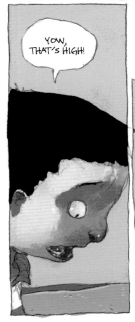

YOW, THAT'S HIGH!

THE STATION AGENT MUST HAVE BEEN WRONG...

TURN AROUND, JOSEPH!!

56

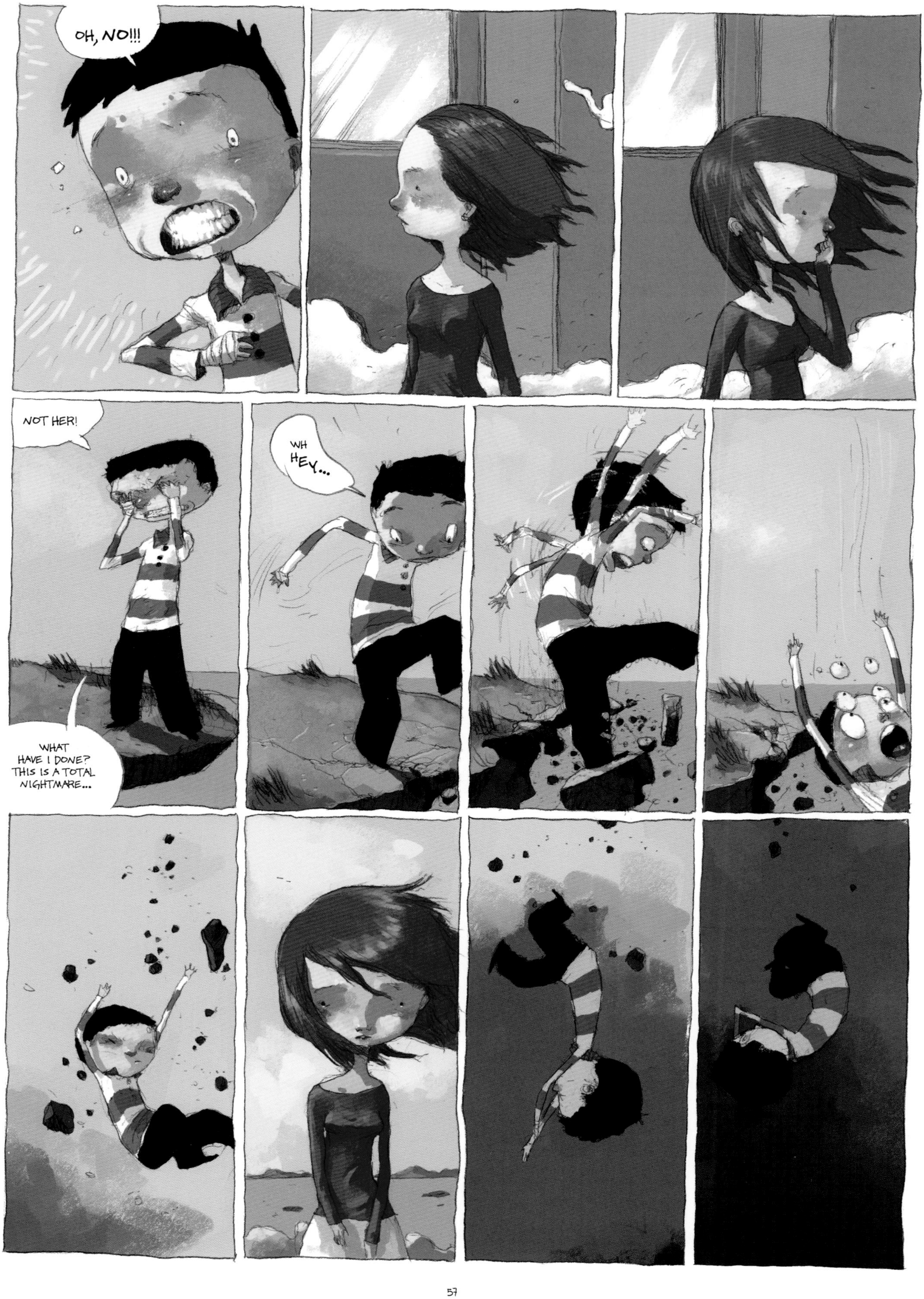
OH, NO!!!
NOT HER!
WHAT HAVE I DONE? THIS IS A TOTAL NIGHTMARE...
WH HEY...

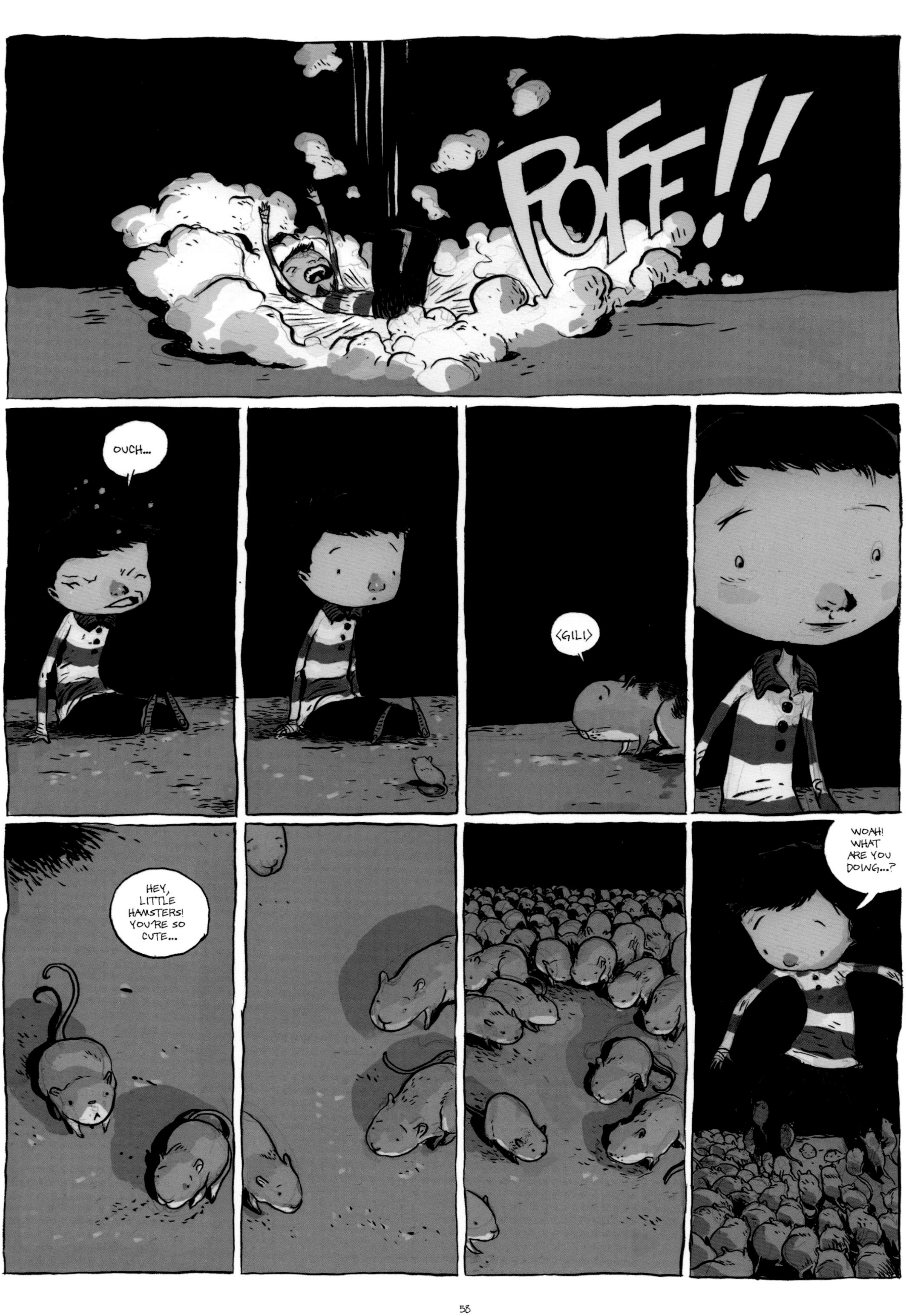
POFF!!
OUCH...
<GILI>
HEY, LITTLE HAMSTERS! YOU'RE SO CUTE...
WOAH! WHAT ARE YOU DOING...?

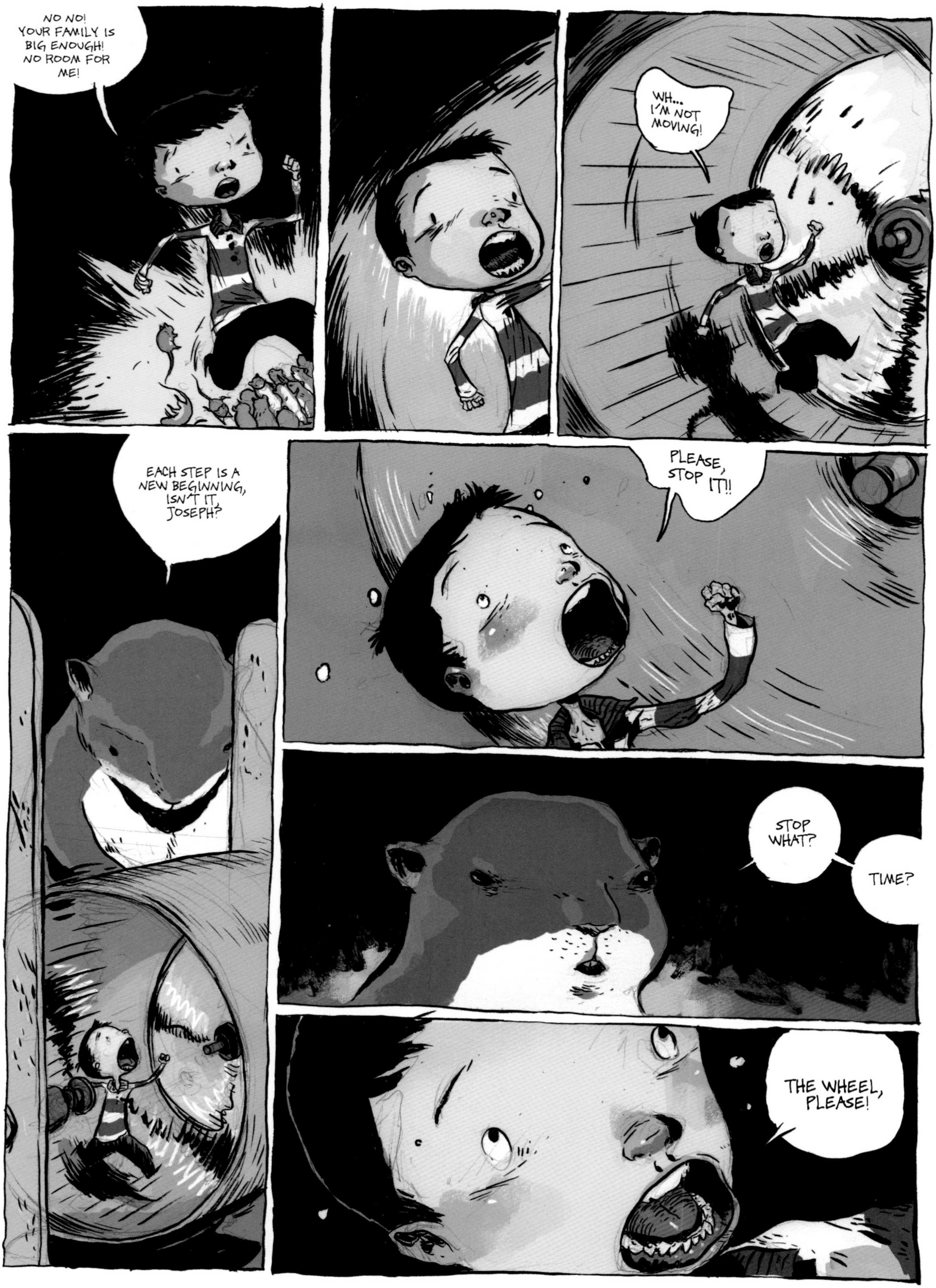
NO NO! YOUR FAMILY IS BIG ENOUGH! NO ROOM FOR ME!
WH... I'M NOT MOVING!
EACH STEP IS A NEW BEGINNING, ISN'T IT, JOSEPH?
PLEASE, STOP IT!!
STOP WHAT?
TIME?
THE WHEEL, PLEASE!

HMMM, IF YOU INSIST...
GOOD LUCK, JOSEPH!
POKE!
BUT REMEMBER...
...HOLD ONTO THE BEAUTIFUL MOMENTS IN LIFE, THOSE TIMES WILL ESCAPE FOREVER.
PAM!
A!
PAF!
A GIANT HAMSTER PREACHING TO ME ABOUT THE VALUE OF TIME... GIMME A BREAK!
GRRRRRR!
OH NO!
NOT AGAIN!!

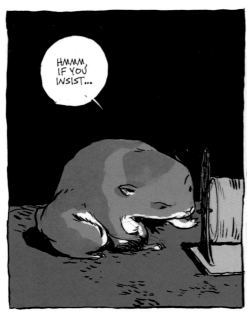

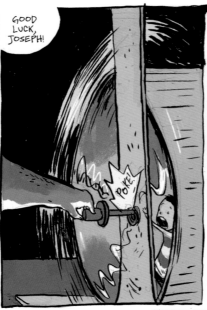

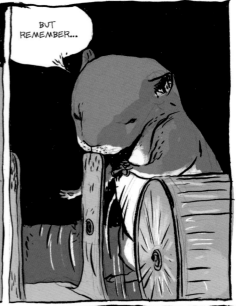

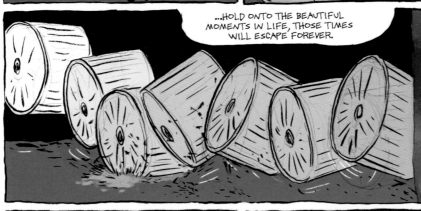

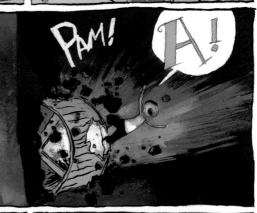

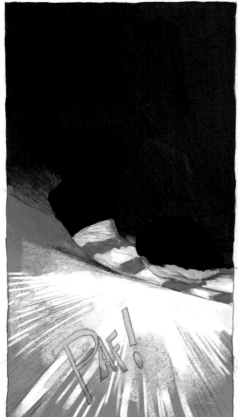

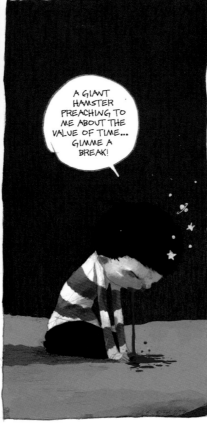

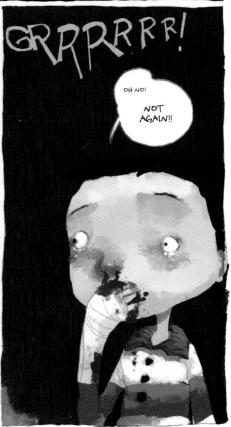

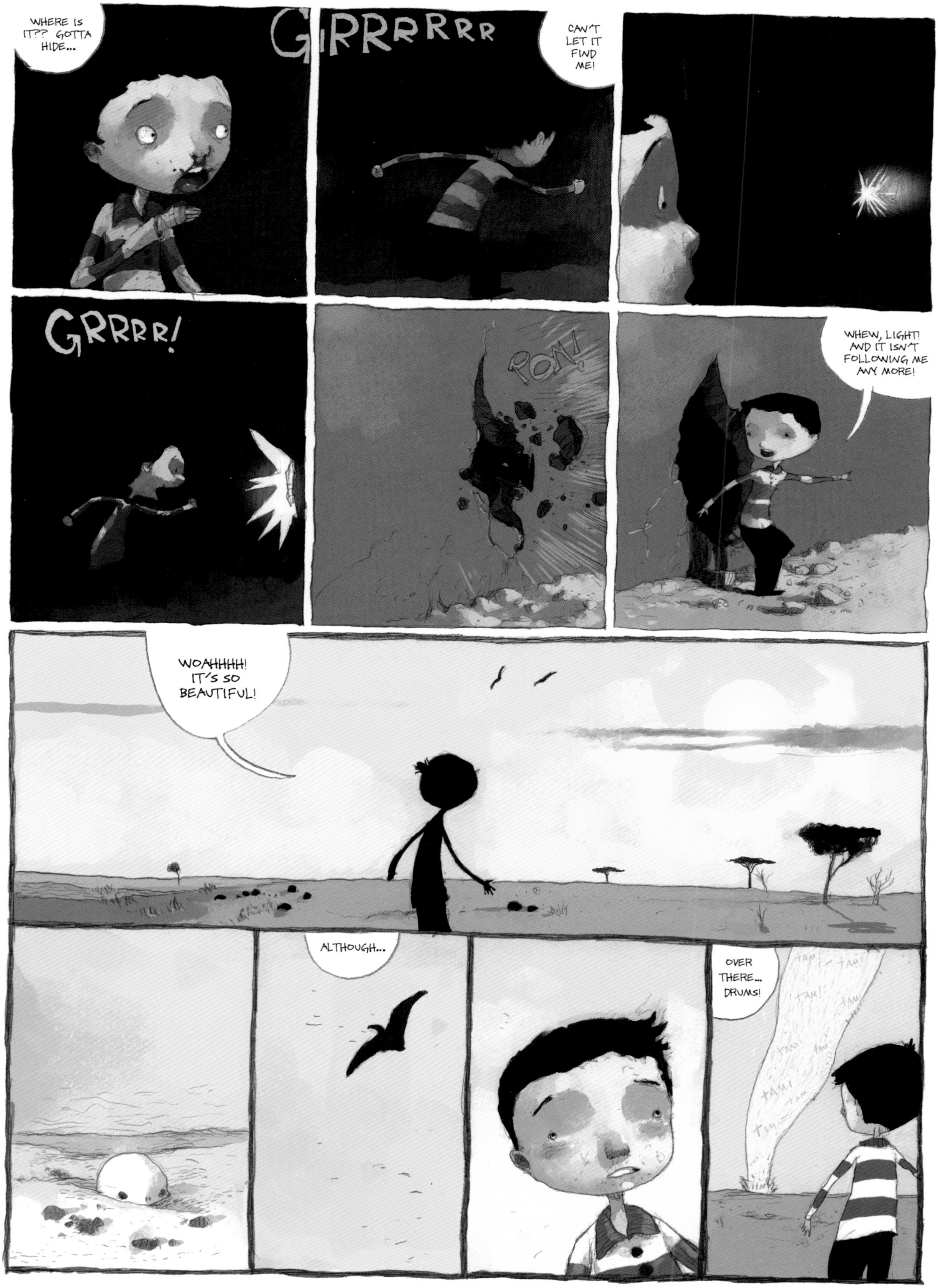
WHERE IS IT?? GOTTA HIDE...
GRRRRRRR
CAN'T LET IT FIND ME!
GRRRR!
POM!
WHEW, LIGHT! AND IT ISN'T FOLLOWING ME ANY MORE!
WOAHHHH! IT'S SO BEAUTIFUL!
ALTHOUGH...
OVER THERE... DRUMS!

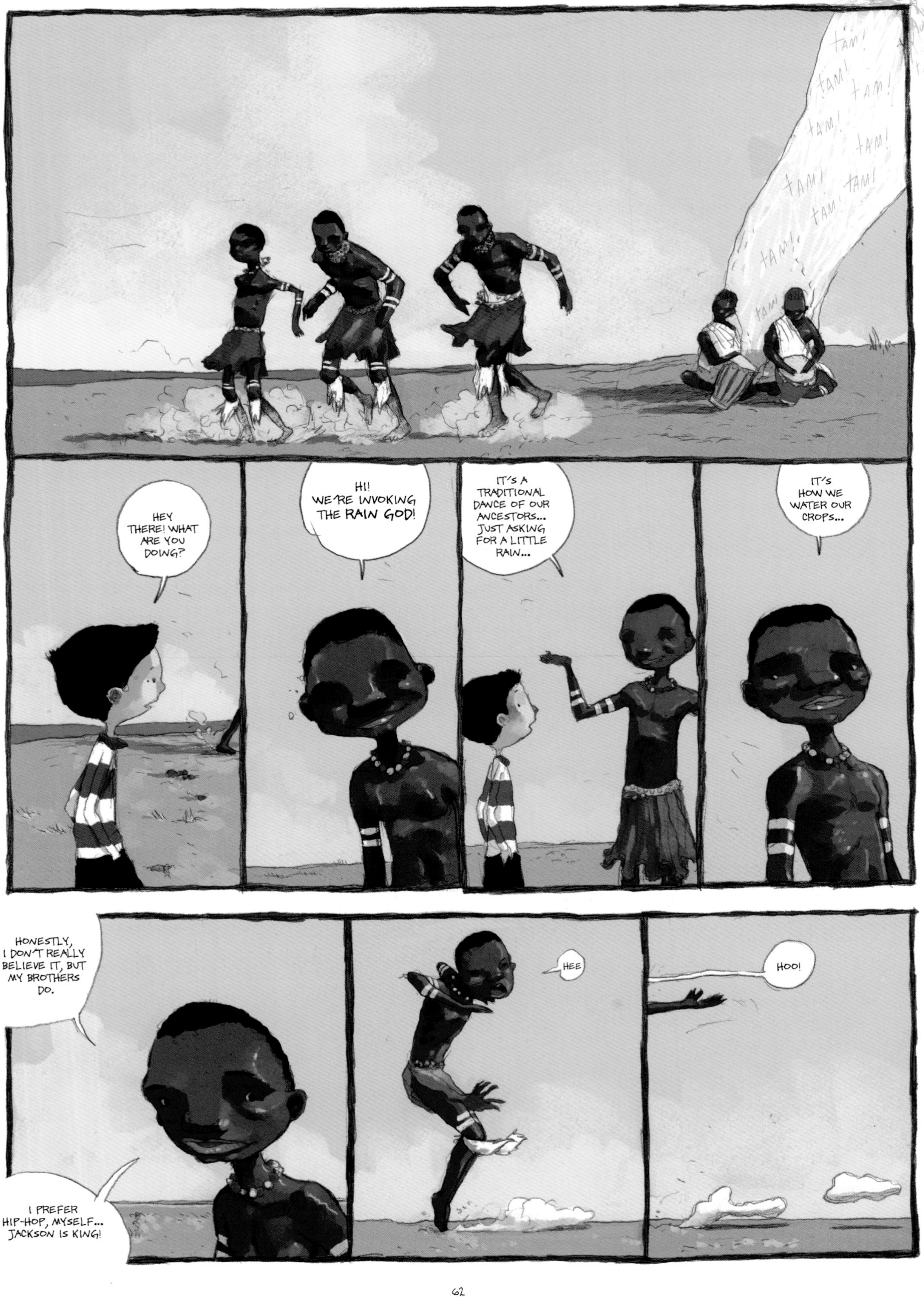
tam! tam! tam! tam! tam! tam! tam! tam! tam!
HEY THERE! WHAT ARE YOU DOING?
HI! WE'RE INVOKING THE RAIN GOD!
IT'S A TRADITIONAL DANCE OF OUR ANCESTORS... JUST ASKING FOR A LITTLE RAIN...
IT'S HOW WE WATER OUR CROPS...
HONESTLY, I DON'T REALLY BELIEVE IT, BUT MY BROTHERS DO.
I PREFER HIP-HOP, MYSELF... JACKSON IS KING!
HEE
HOO!

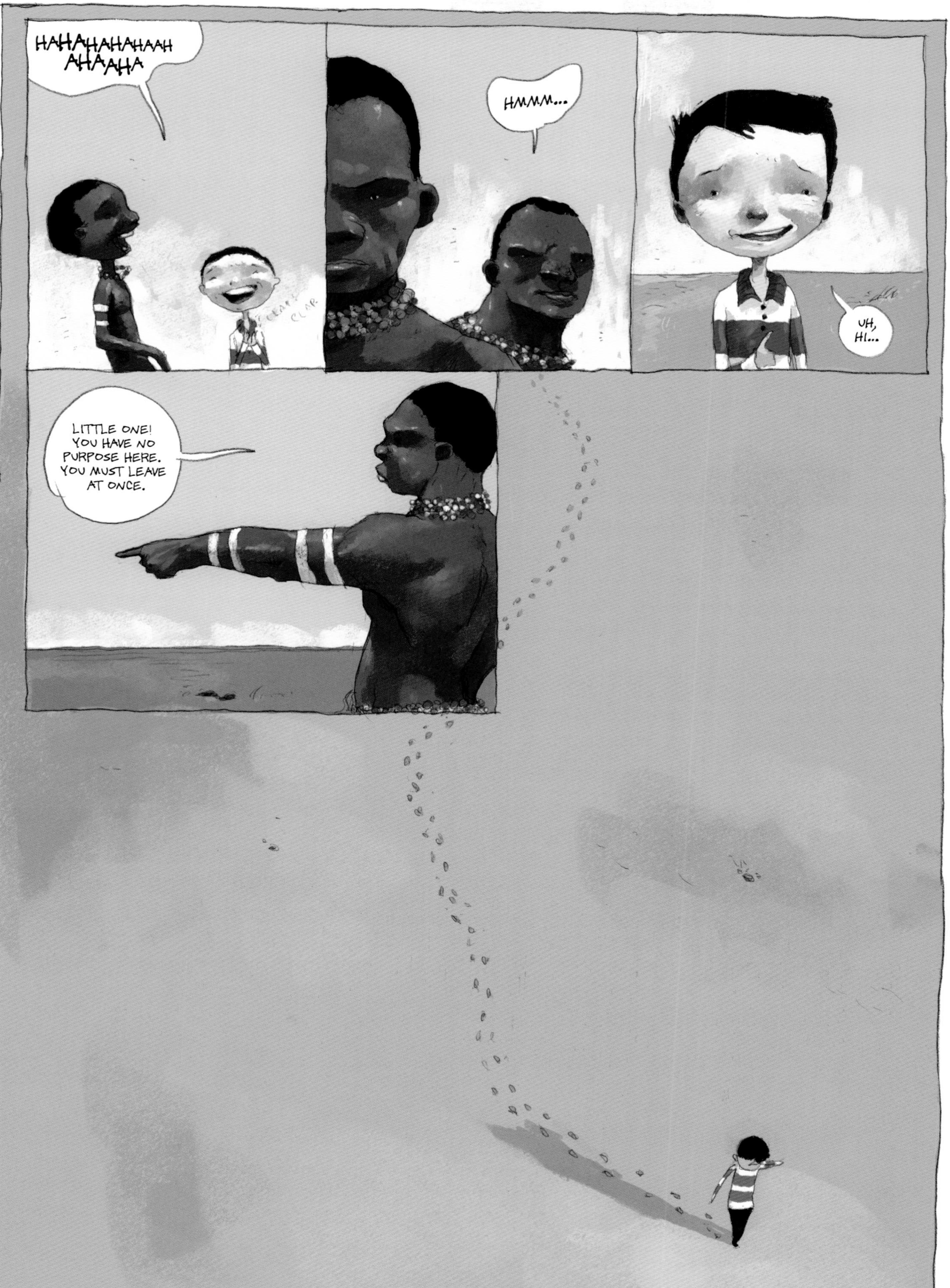
HAHAHAHAHAAH AHAAHA
CLAP CLAP
HMMM...
UH, HI...
LITTLE ONE! YOU HAVE NO PURPOSE HERE. YOU MUST LEAVE AT ONCE.

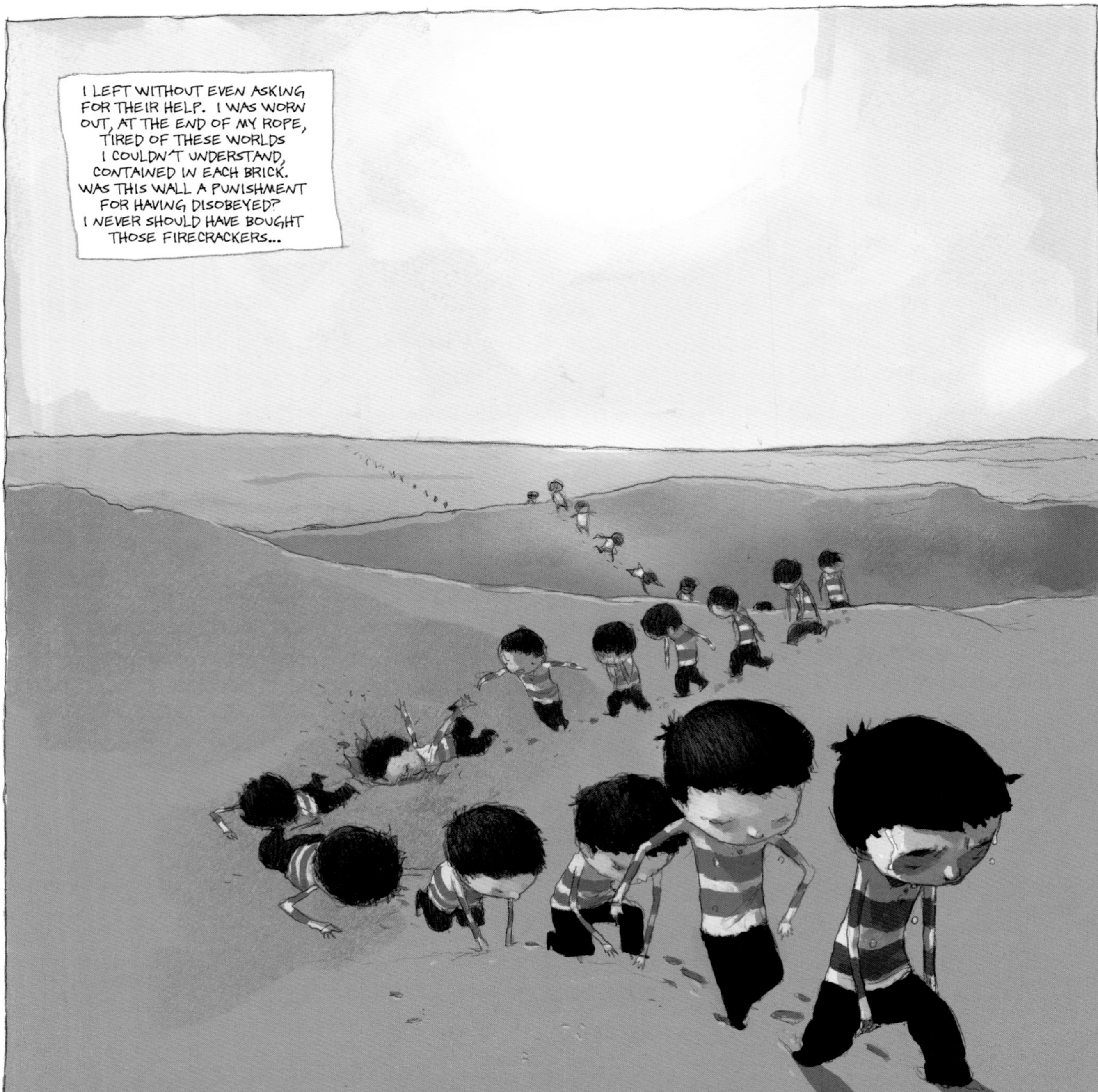
I LEFT WITHOUT EVEN ASKING FOR THEIR HELP. I WAS WORN OUT, AT THE END OF MY ROPE, TIRED OF THESE WORLDS I COULDN'T UNDERSTAND, CONTAINED IN EACH BRICK. WAS THIS WALL A PUNISHMENT FOR HAVING DISOBEYED? I NEVER SHOULD HAVE BOUGHT THOSE FIRECRACKERS...

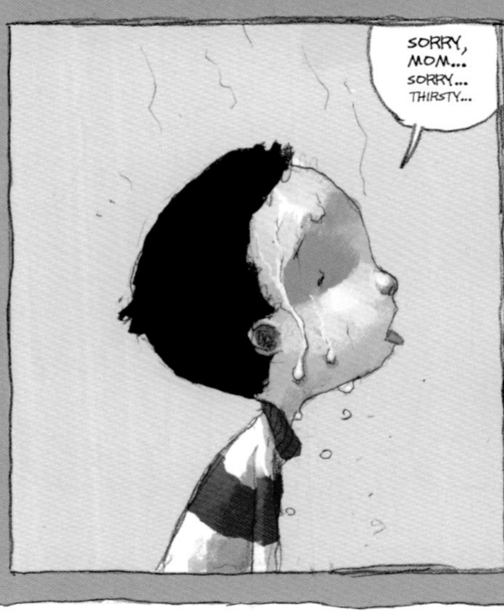
SORRY, MOM... SORRY... THIRSTY...

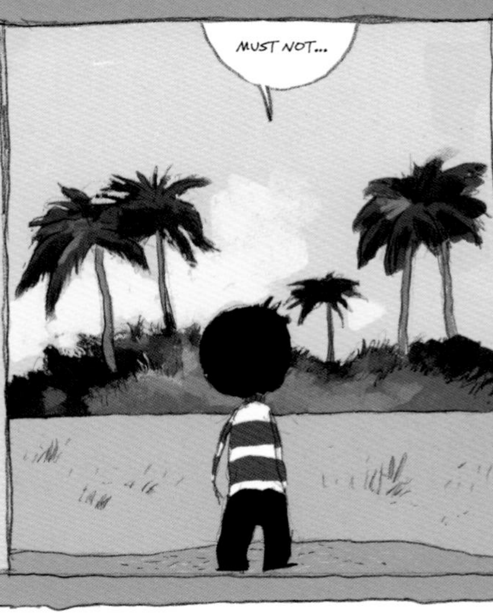
MUST NOT...

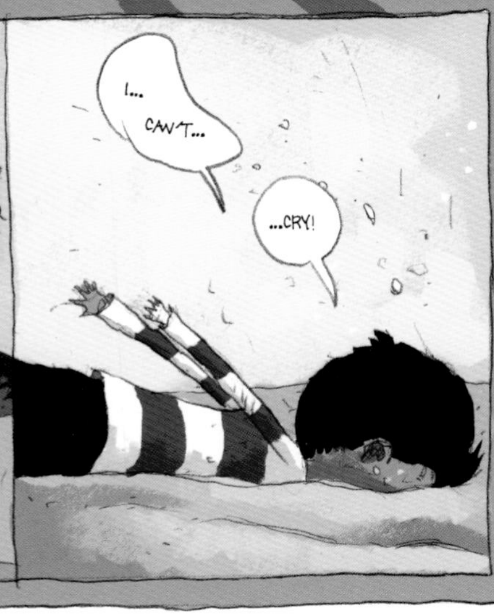
I... CAN'T...
...CRY!

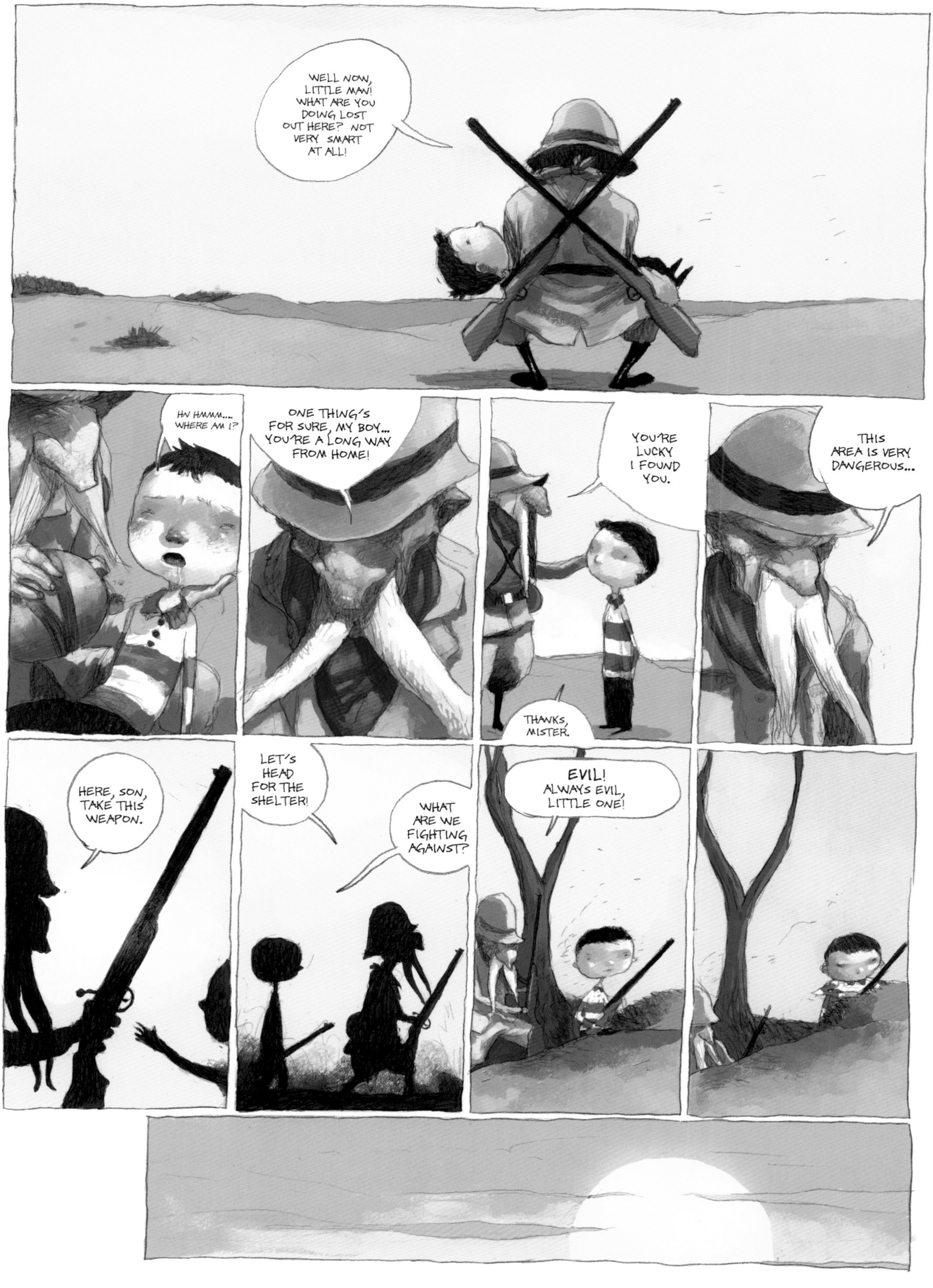
WELL NOW, LITTLE MAN! WHAT ARE YOU DOING LOST OUT HERE? NOT VERY SMART AT ALL!
HN HMMM... WHERE AM I?
ONE THING'S FOR SURE, MY BOY... YOU'RE A LONG WAY FROM HOME!
YOU'RE LUCKY I FOUND YOU.
THANKS, MISTER.
THIS AREA IS VERY DANGEROUS...
HERE, SON, TAKE THIS WEAPON.
LET'S HEAD FOR THE SHELTER!
WHAT ARE WE FIGHTING AGAINST?
EVIL! ALWAYS EVIL, LITTLE ONE!

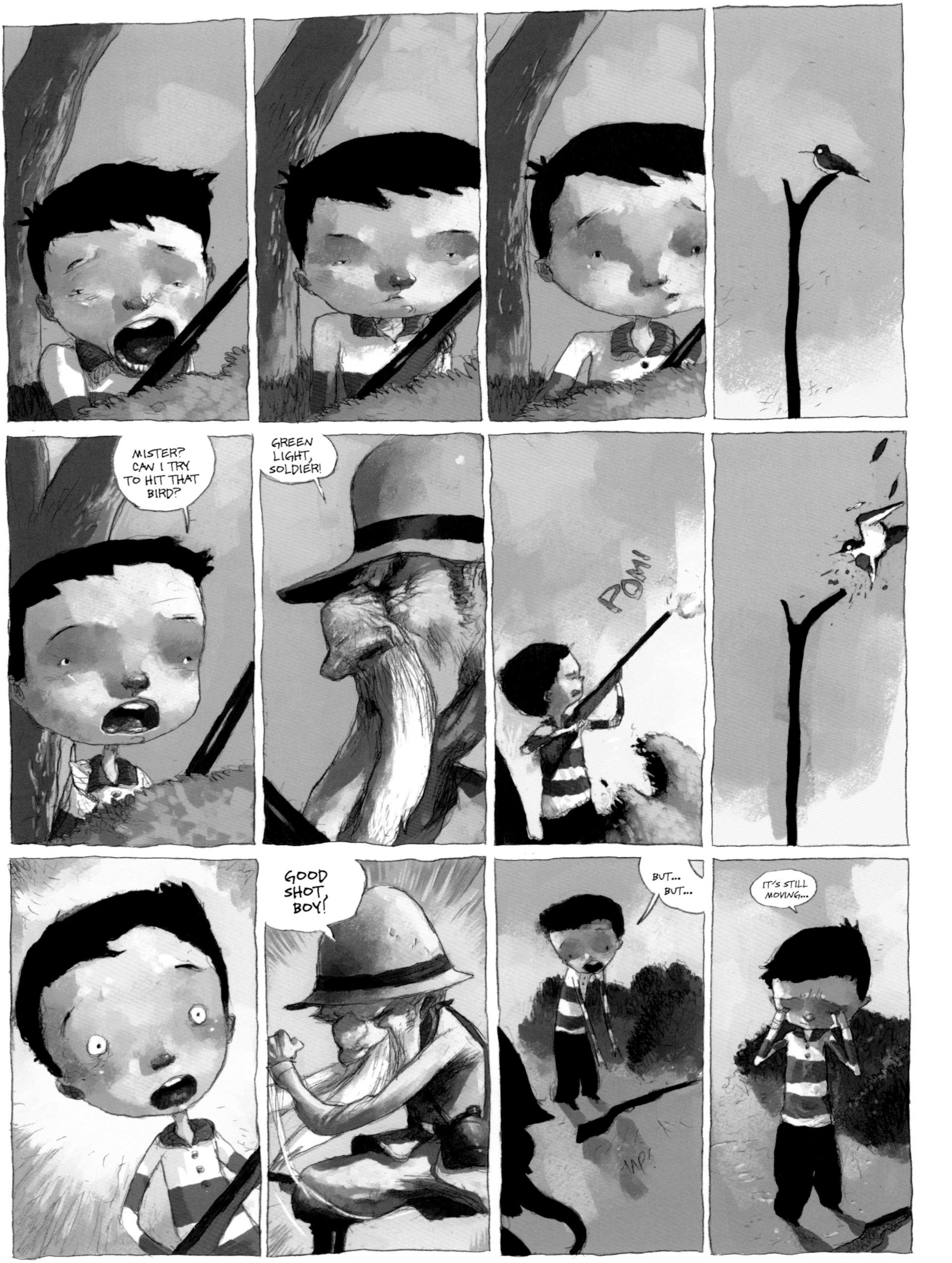
MISTER? CAN I TRY TO HIT THAT BIRD?
GREEN LIGHT, SOLDIER!
POM!
GOOD SHOT, BOY!
BUT... BUT...
IT'S STILL MOVING...

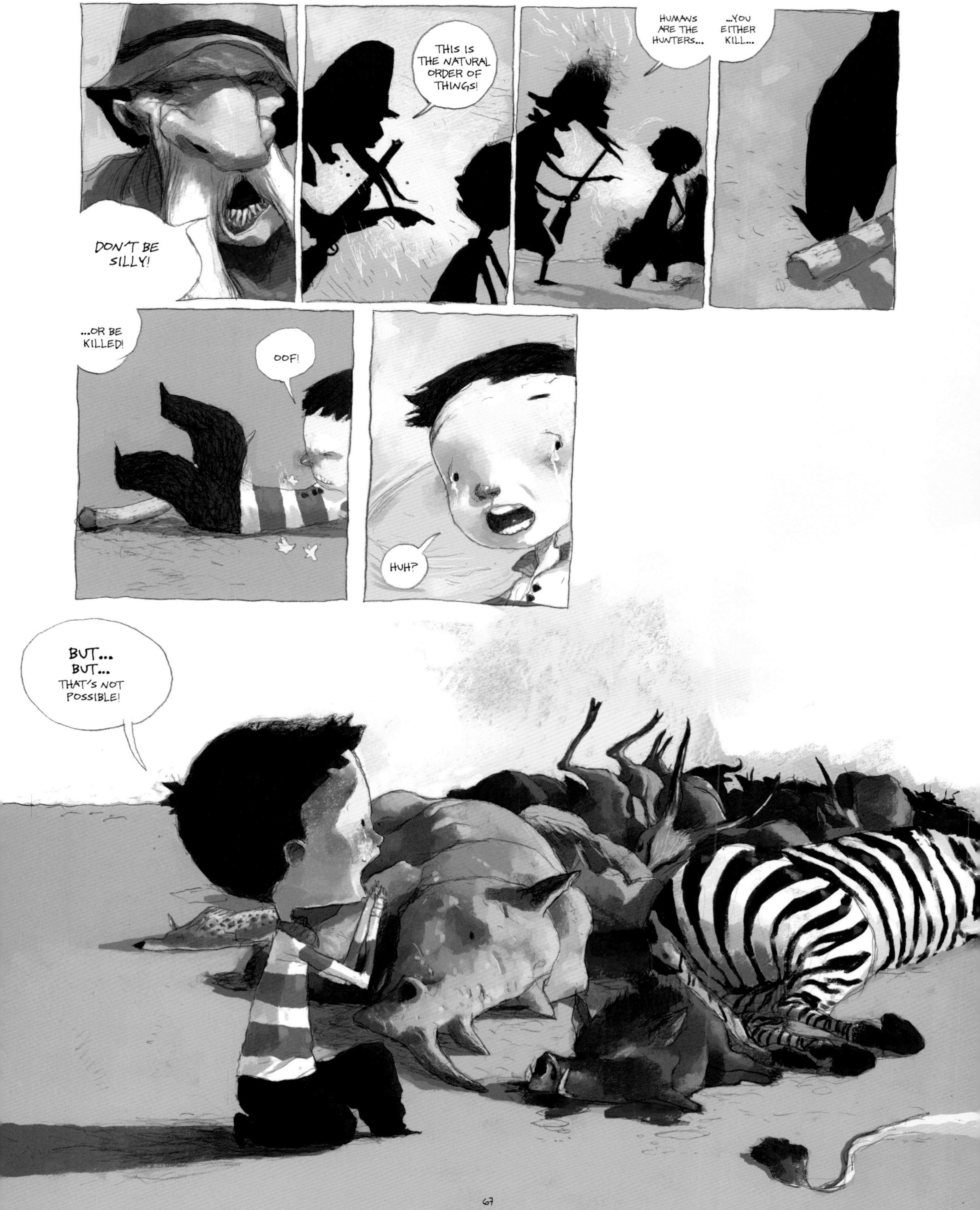
DON'T BE SILLY!
THIS IS THE NATURAL ORDER OF THINGS!
HUMANS ARE THE HUNTERS...
...YOU EITHER KILL...
...OR BE KILLED!
OOF!
HUH?
BUT... BUT... THAT'S NOT POSSIBLE!

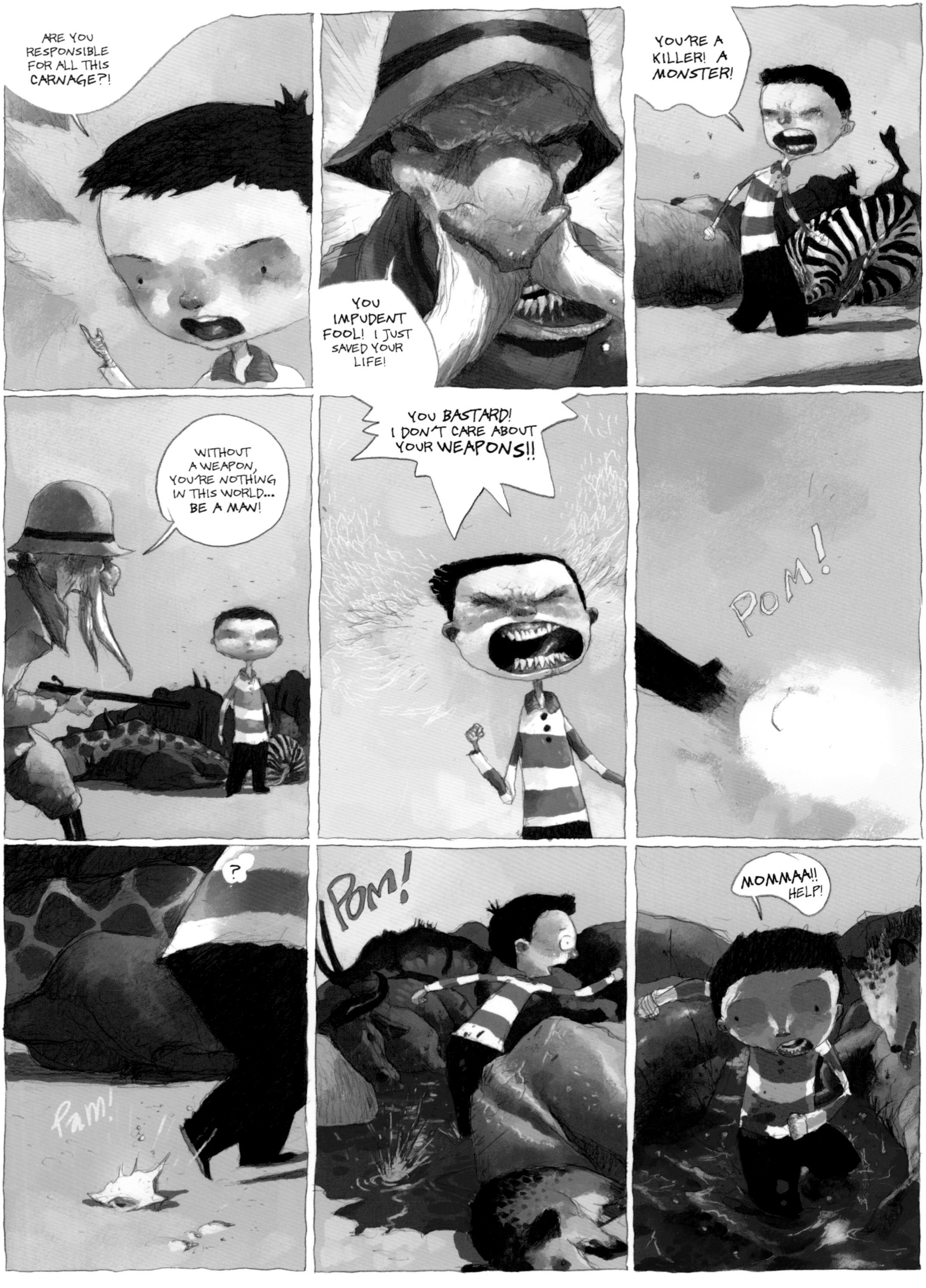
ARE YOU RESPONSIBLE FOR ALL THIS CARNAGE?!
YOU IMPUDENT FOOL! I JUST SAVED YOUR LIFE!
YOU'RE A KILLER! A MONSTER!
WITHOUT A WEAPON, YOU'RE NOTHING IN THIS WORLD... BE A MAN!
YOU BASTARD! I DON'T CARE ABOUT YOUR WEAPONS!!
POM!
?
PAM!
POM!
MOMMAA!! HELP!

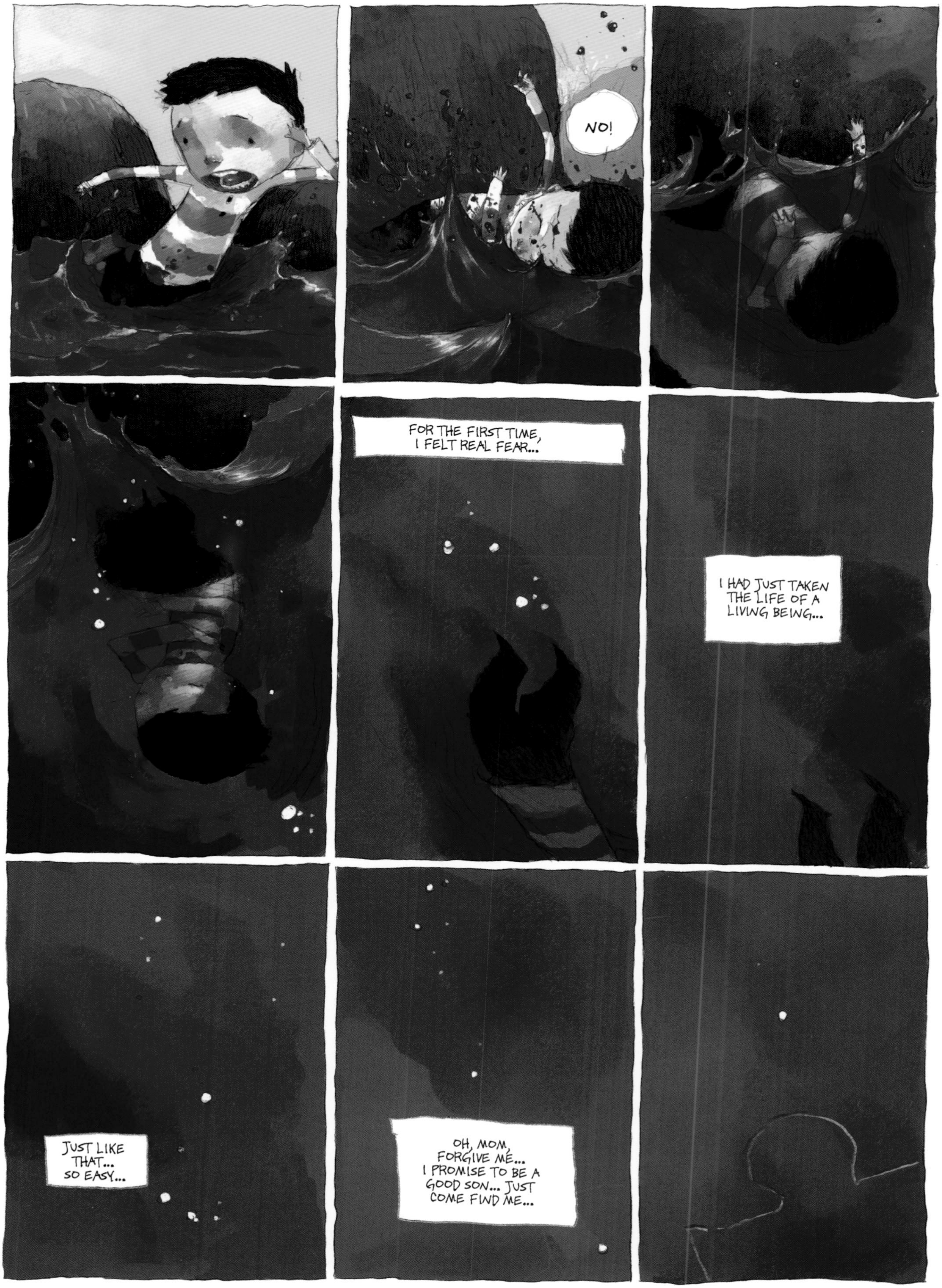
NO!
FOR THE FIRST TIME, I FELT REAL FEAR...
I HAD JUST TAKEN THE LIFE OF A LIVING BEING...
JUST LIKE THAT... SO EASY...
OH, MOM, FORGIVE ME... I PROMISE TO BE A GOOD SON... JUST COME FIND ME...

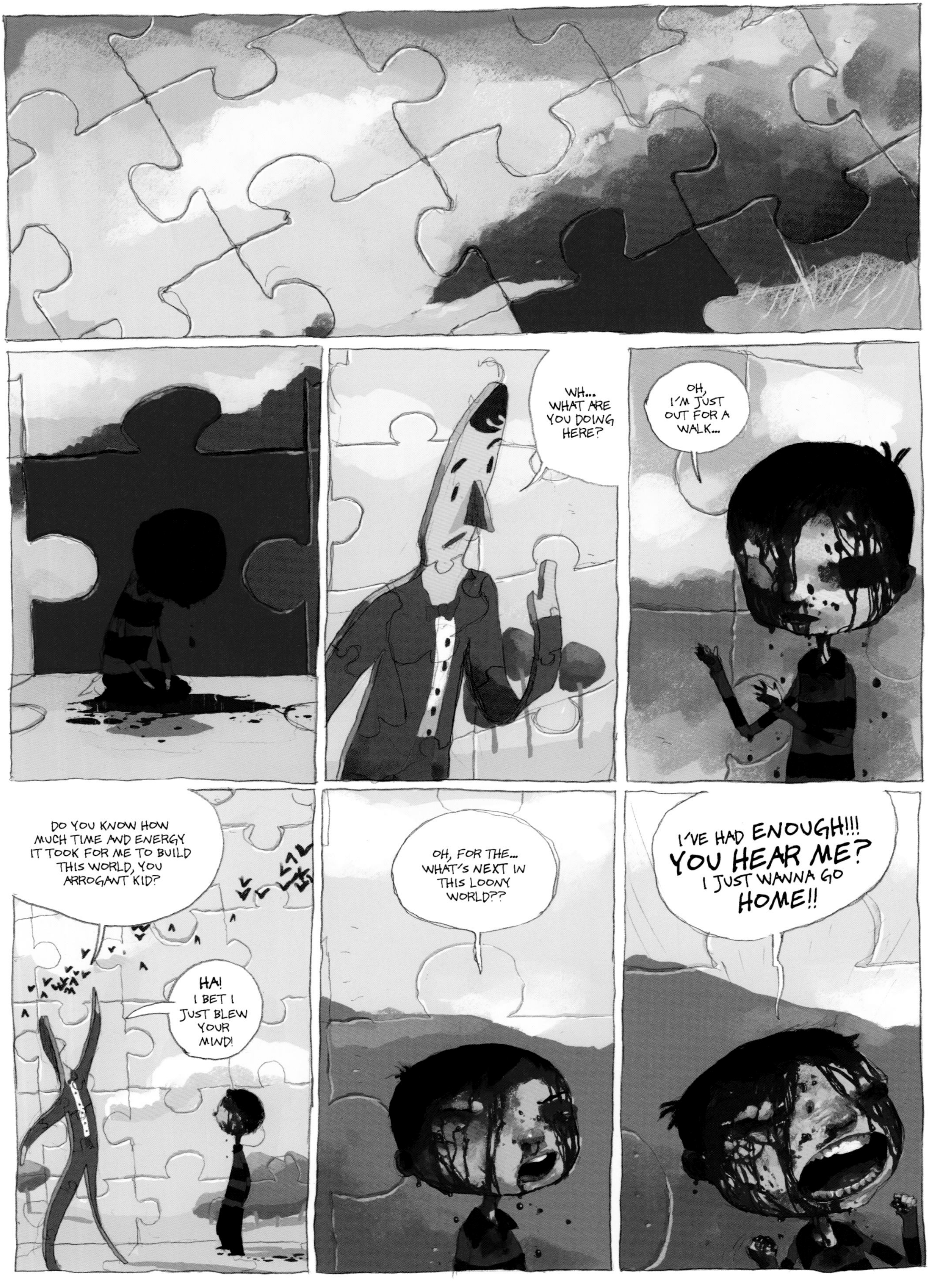
WH... WHAT ARE YOU DOING HERE?
OH, I'M JUST OUT FOR A WALK...
DO YOU KNOW HOW MUCH TIME AND ENERGY IT TOOK FOR ME TO BUILD THIS WORLD, YOU ARROGANT KID?
HA! I BET I JUST BLEW YOUR MIND!
OH, FOR THE... WHAT'S NEXT IN THIS LOONY WORLD??
I'VE HAD ENOUGH!!! YOU HEAR ME? I JUST WANNA GO HOME!!

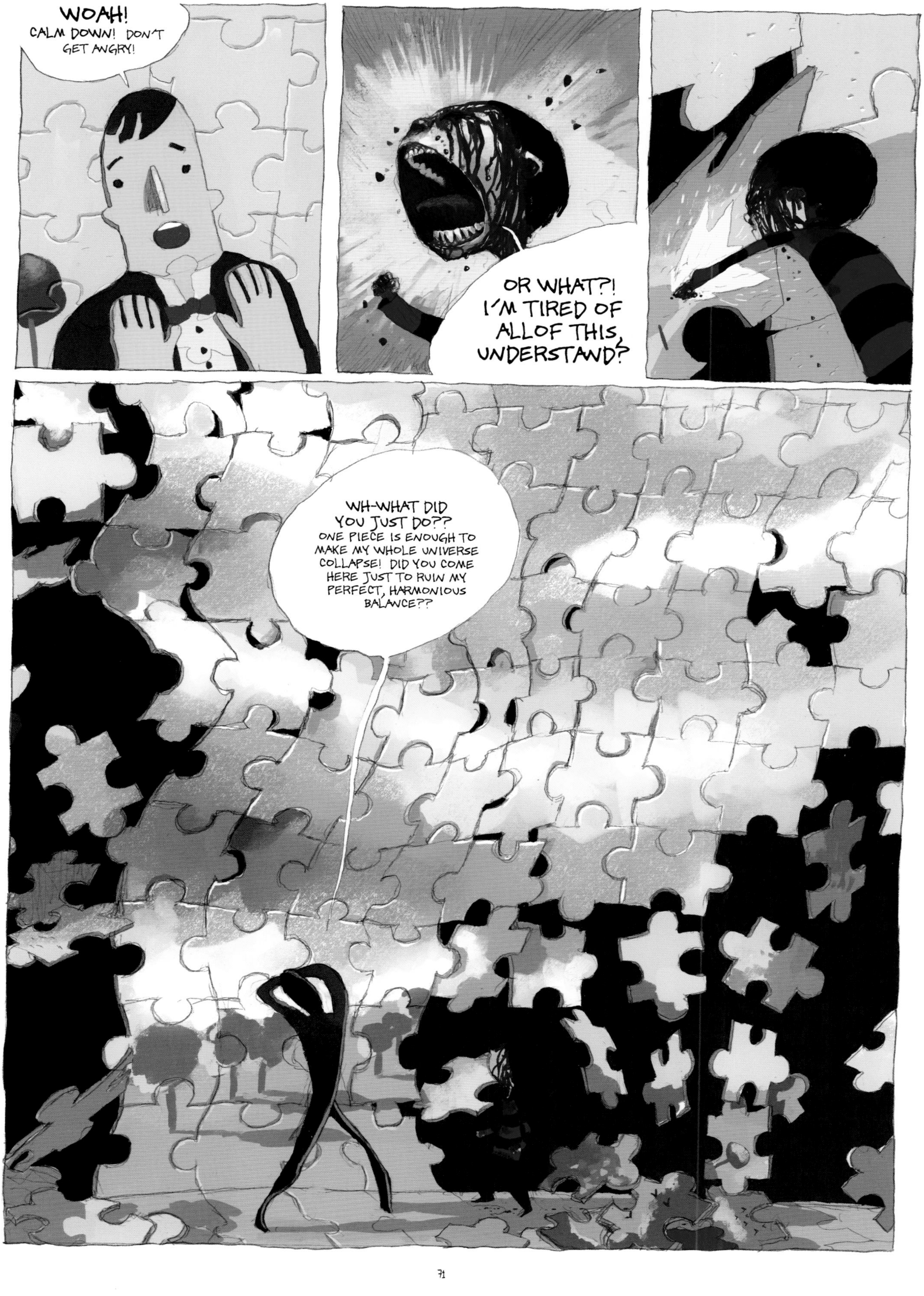
WOAH! CALM DOWN! DON'T GET ANGRY!
OR WHAT?! I'M TIRED OF ALL OF THIS, UNDERSTAND?
WH-WHAT DID YOU JUST DO?? ONE PIECE IS ENOUGH TO MAKE MY WHOLE UNIVERSE COLLAPSE! DID YOU COME HERE JUST TO RUIN MY PERFECT, HARMONIOUS BALANCE??

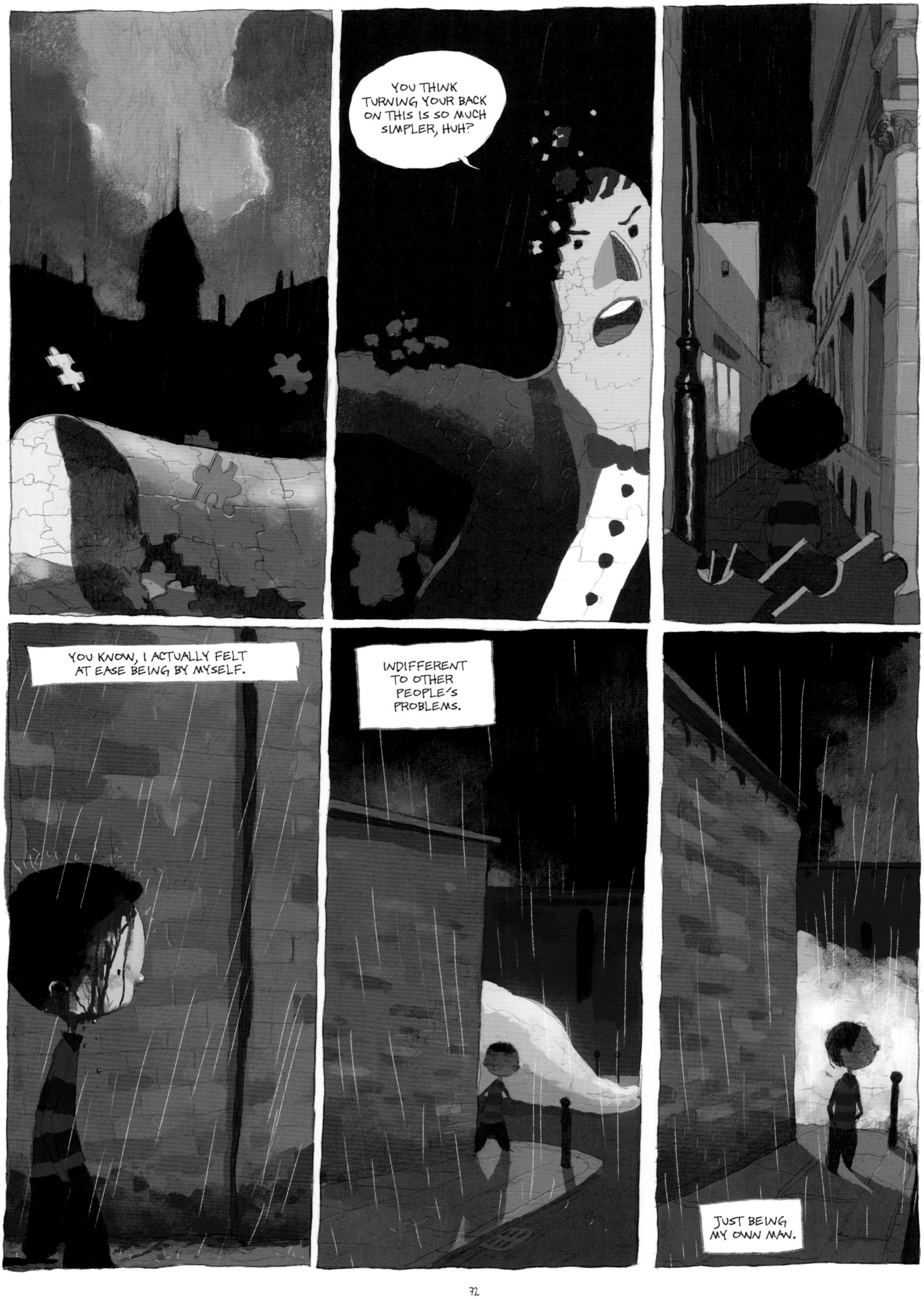
YOU THINK TURNING YOUR BACK ON THIS IS SO MUCH SIMPLER, HUH?
YOU KNOW, I ACTUALLY FELT AT EASE BEING BY MYSELF.
INDIFFERENT TO OTHER PEOPLE'S PROBLEMS.
JUST BEING MY OWN MAN.

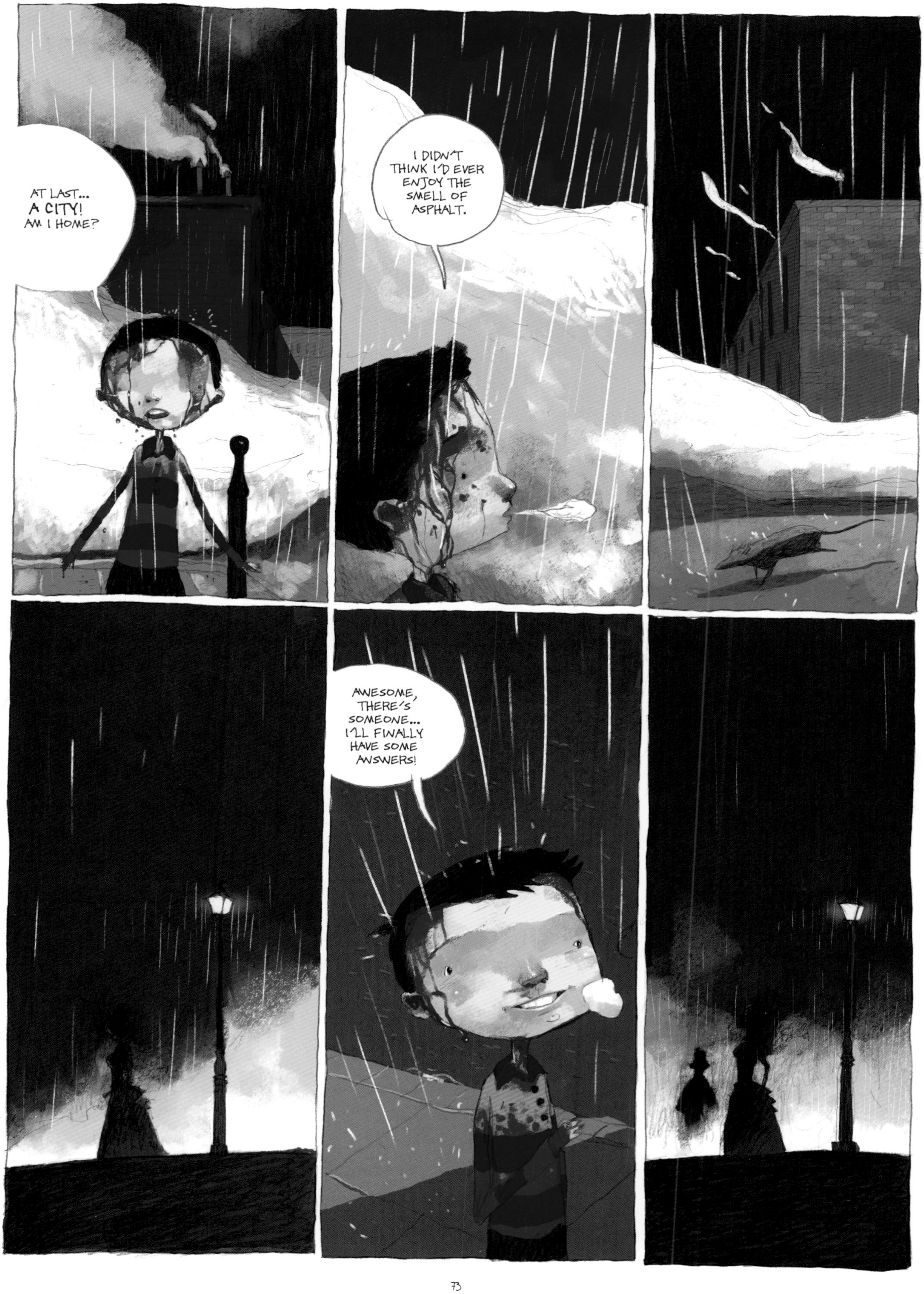
AT LAST... A CITY! AM I HOME?
I DIDN'T THINK I'D EVER ENJOY THE SMELL OF ASPHALT.
AWESOME, THERE'S SOMEONE... I'LL FINALLY HAVE SOME ANSWERS!

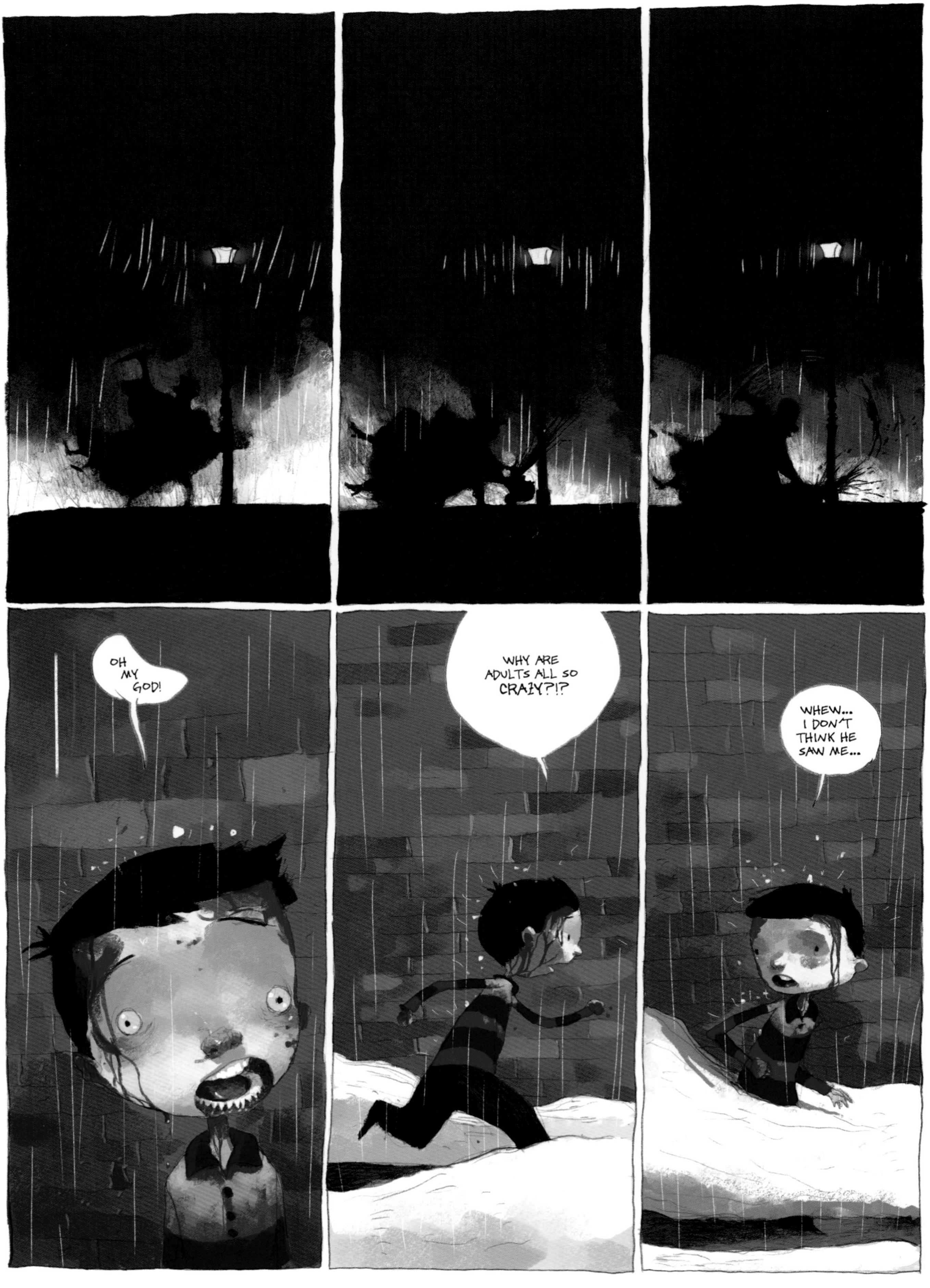
OH MY GOD!
WHY ARE ADULTS ALL SO CRAZY?!?
WHEW... I DON'T THINK HE SAW ME...

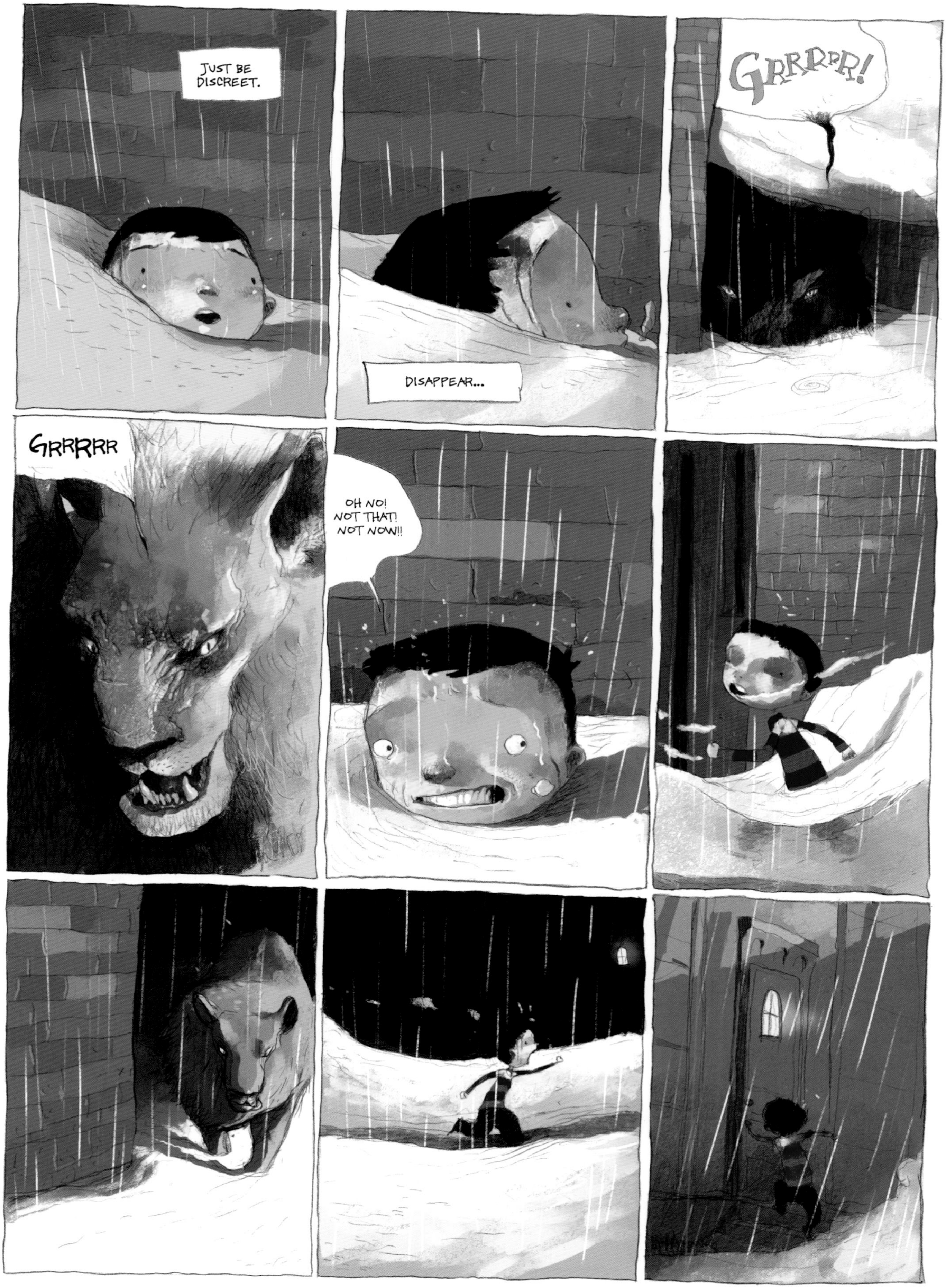
JUST BE DISCREET.
DISAPPEAR...
GRRRRR!
GRRRRR
OH NO! NOT THAT! NOT NOW!!

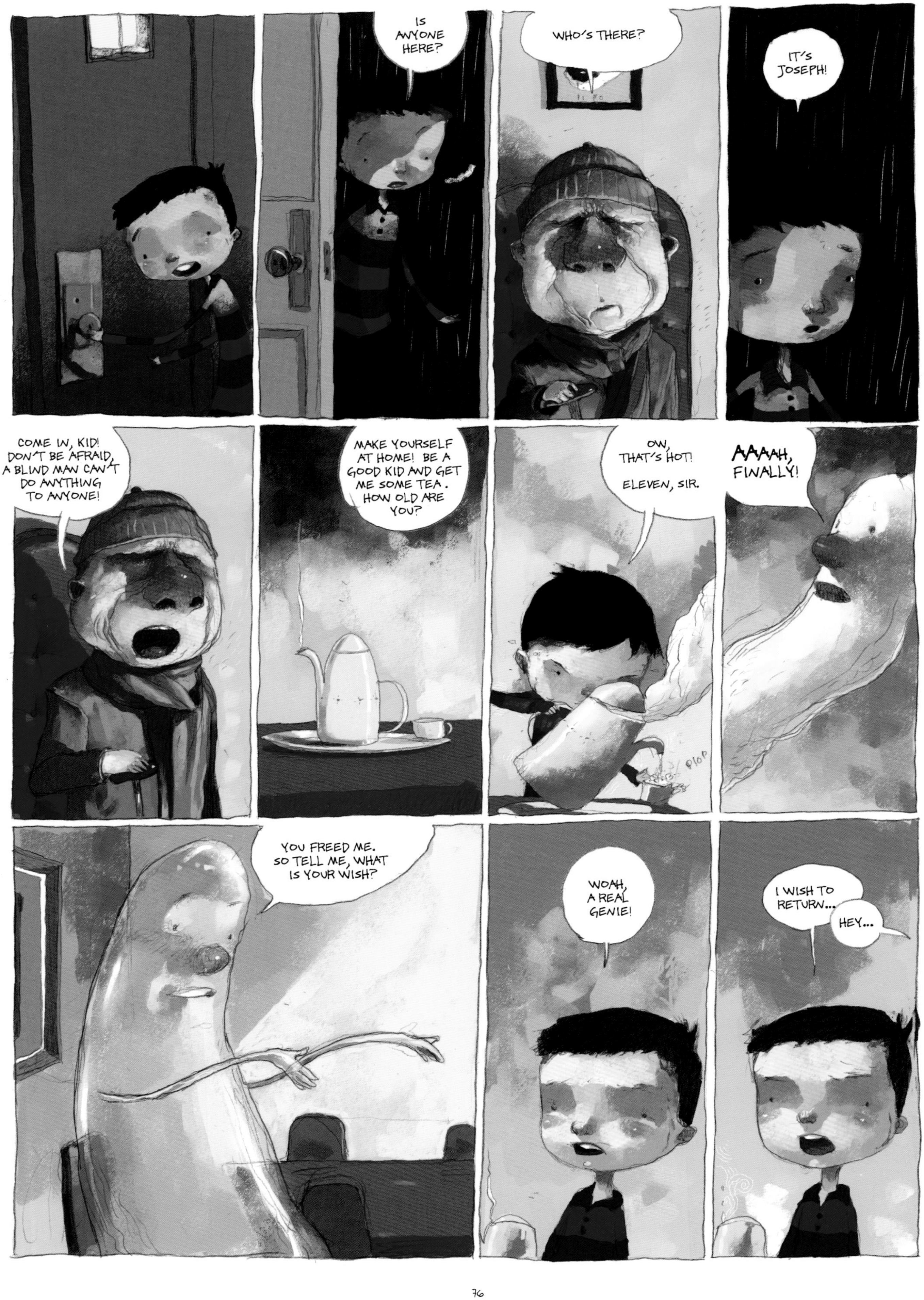
IS ANYONE HERE?
WHO'S THERE?
IT'S JOSEPH!
COME IN, KID! DON'T BE AFRAID, A BLIND MAN CAN'T DO ANYTHING TO ANYONE!
MAKE YOURSELF AT HOME! BE A GOOD KID AND GET ME SOME TEA. HOW OLD ARE YOU?
OW, THAT'S HOT!
ELEVEN, SIR.
PLOP
AAAAH, FINALLY!
YOU FREED ME. SO TELL ME, WHAT IS YOUR WISH?
WOAH, A REAL GENIE!
I WISH TO RETURN...
HEY...

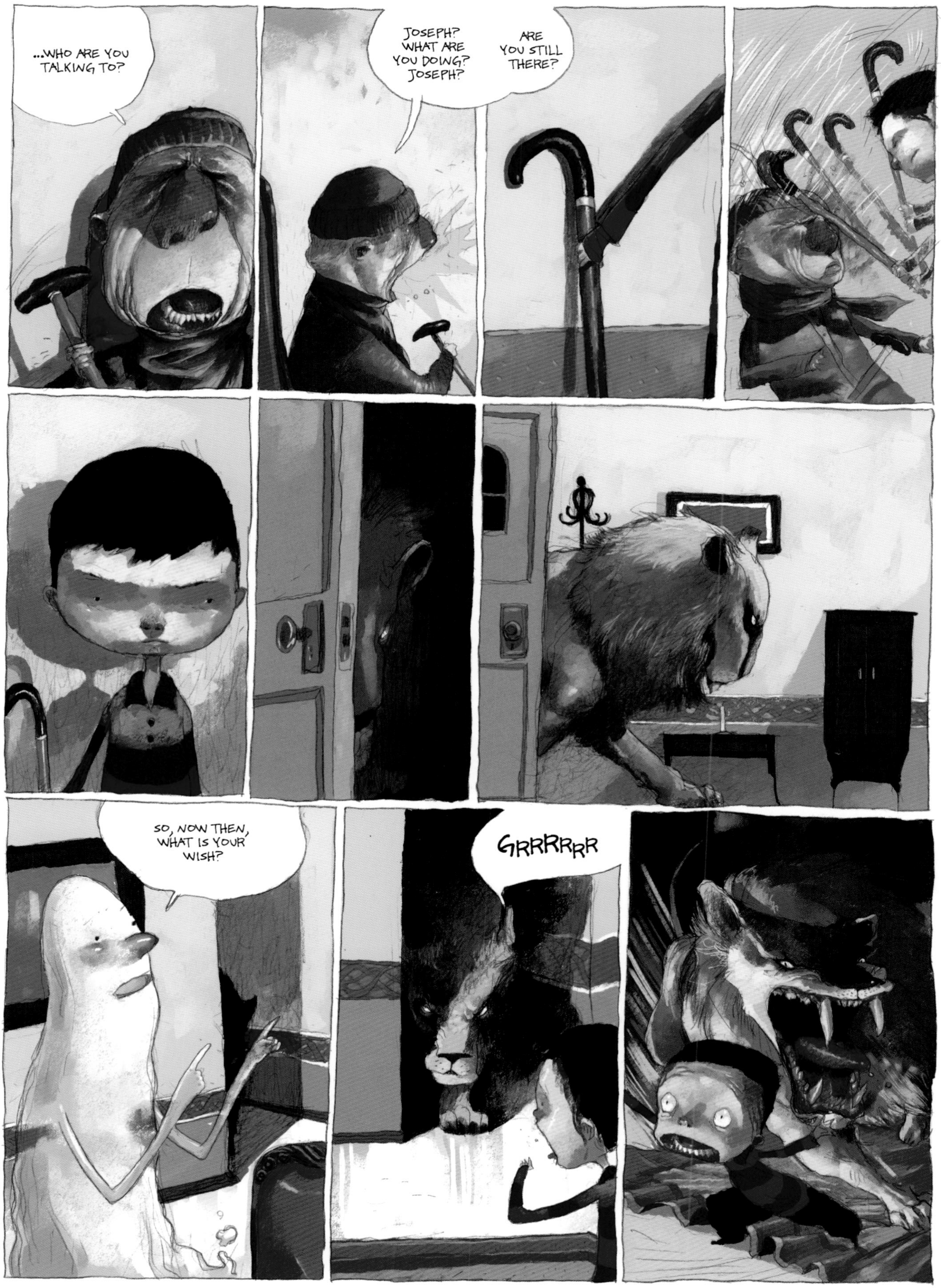
...WHO ARE YOU TALKING TO?
JOSEPH? WHAT ARE YOU DOING? JOSEPH?
ARE YOU STILL THERE?
SO, NOW THEN, WHAT IS YOUR WISH?
GRRRRRR

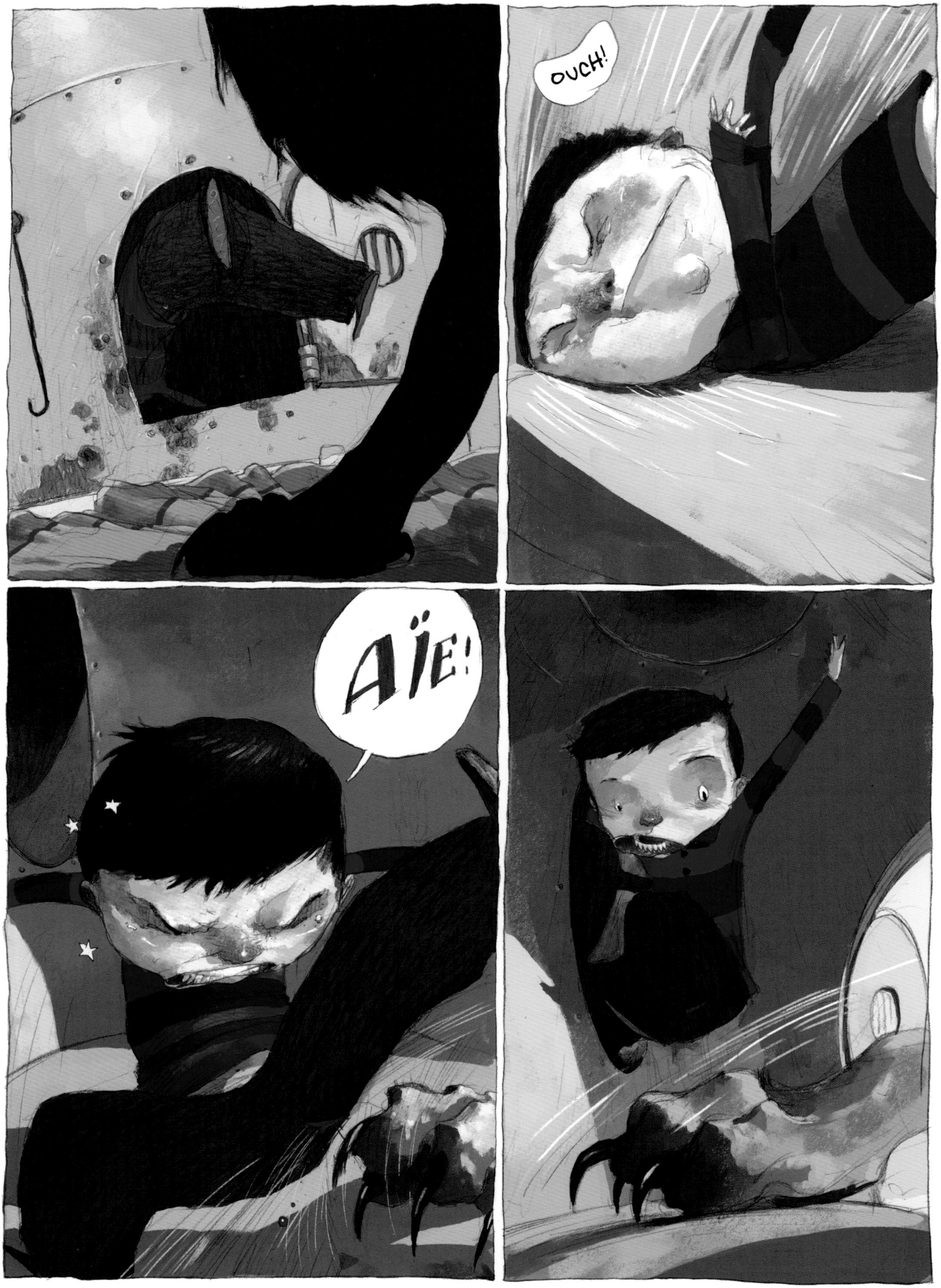
OUCH!
AÏE!

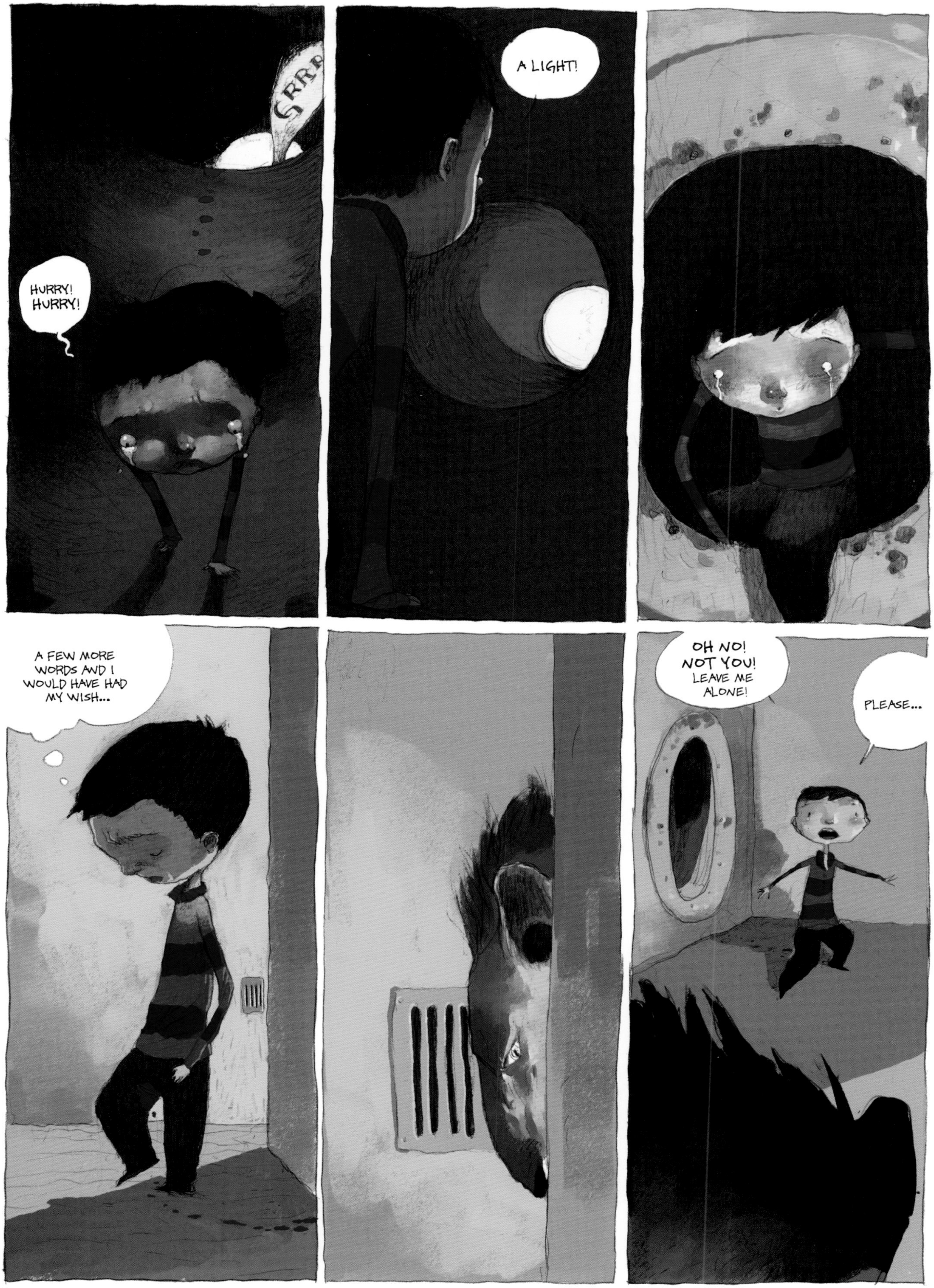
GRRR
HURRY! HURRY!
A LIGHT!
A FEW MORE WORDS AND I WOULD HAVE HAD MY WISH...
OH NO! NOT YOU! LEAVE ME ALONE!
PLEASE...

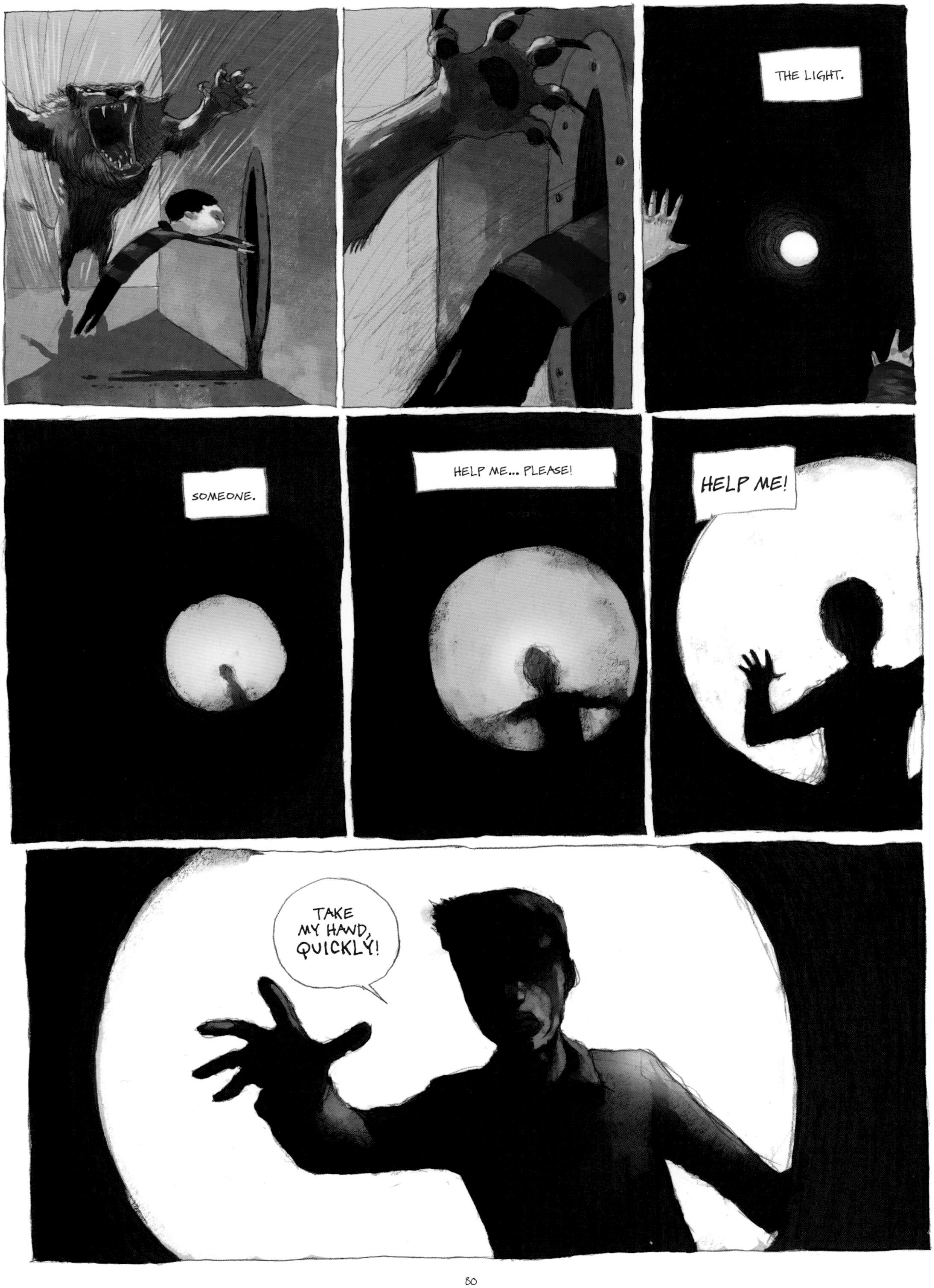
THE LIGHT.
SOMEONE.
HELP ME... PLEASE!
HELP ME!
TAKE MY HAND, QUICKLY!

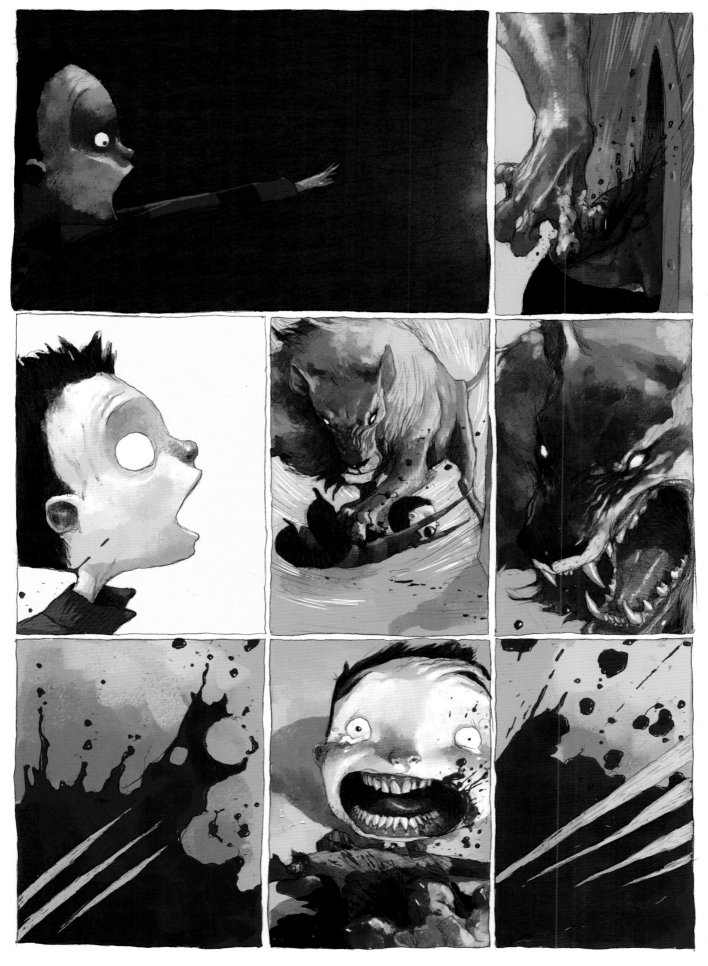

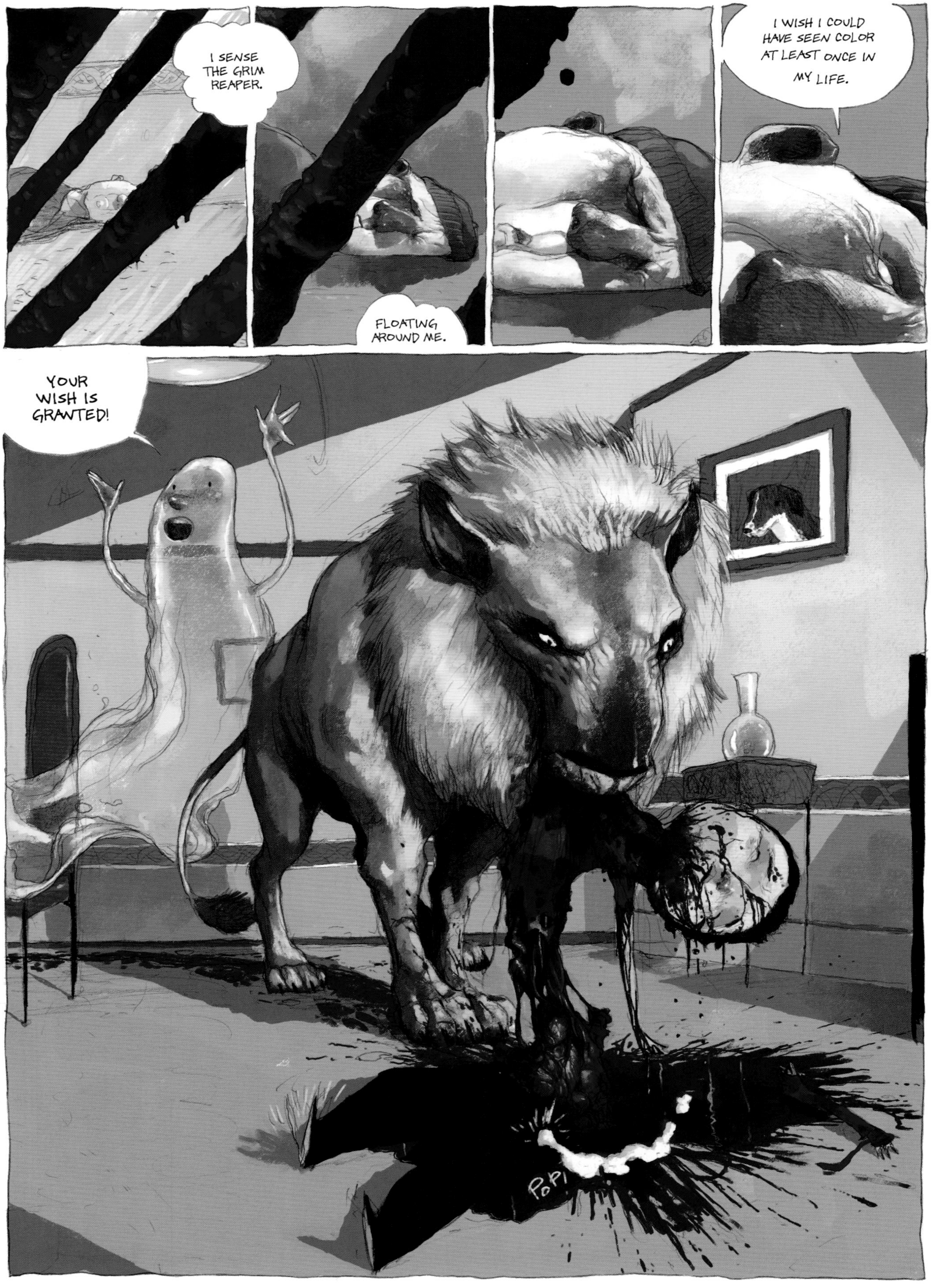
I SENSE THE GRIM REAPER.
FLOATING AROUND ME.
I WISH I COULD HAVE SEEN COLOR AT LEAST ONCE IN MY LIFE.
YOUR WISH IS GRANTED!
POP!

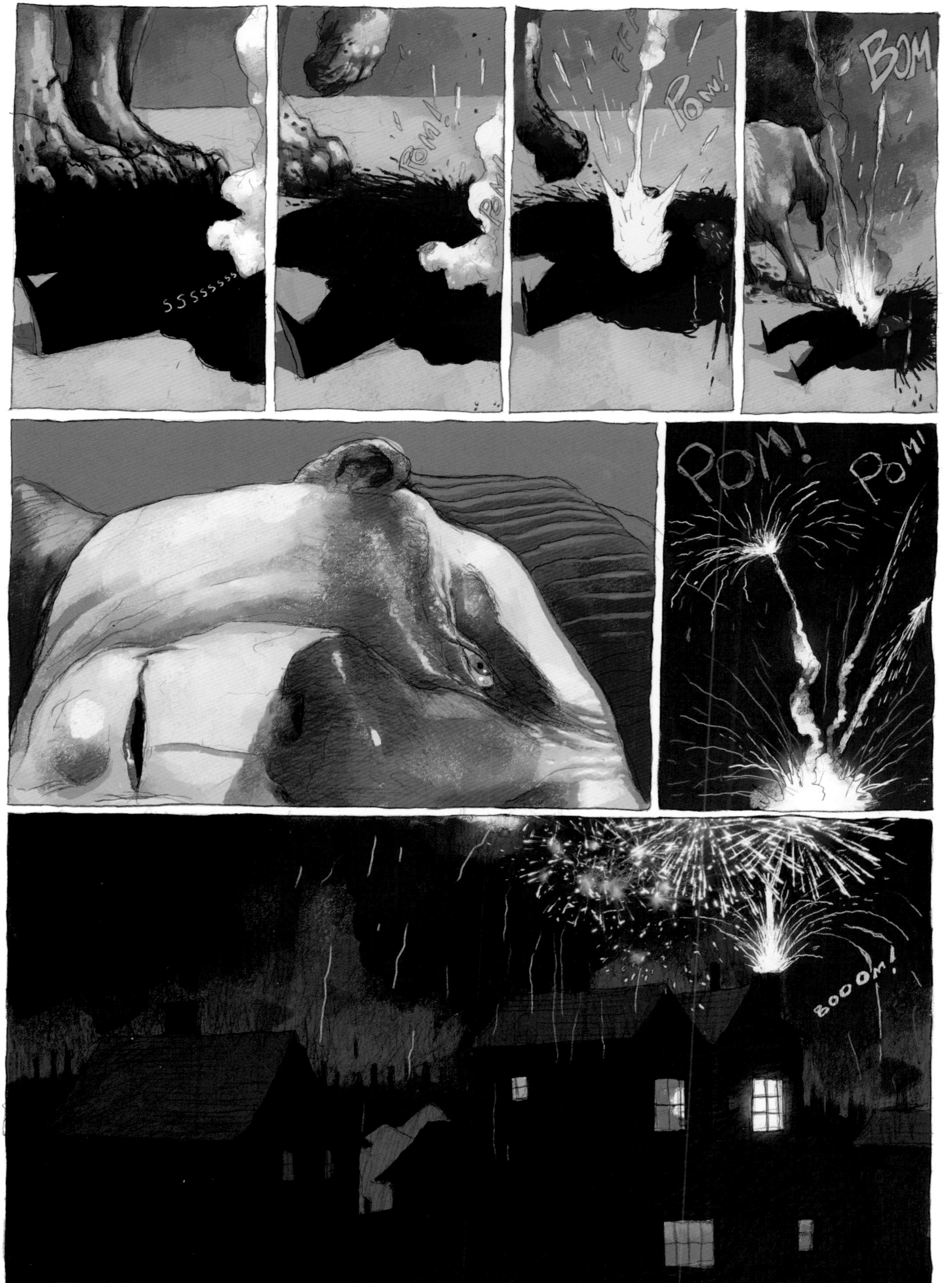
SSSSSSS
POM!
POM!
POM!
BOM
POM!
POM!
BOOOM!

I'M ELEVEN
YEARS OLD...

MY NAME
IS JOSEPH...

AND I HAVE
DECIDED TO LIVE...

I LOOKED DOWN AT THE GLASS
TABLE IN FRONT OF ME...

I REFRAINED FROM JUMPING
THROUGH IT HEAD FIRST...
LIVE OR DIE...
I MADE MY DECISION...

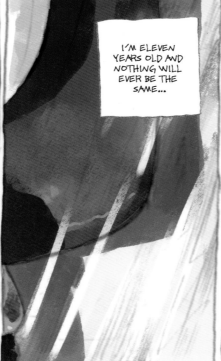

I'M ELEVEN
YEARS OLD AND
NOTHING WILL
EVER BE THE
SAME...

I BECAME A MAN
WITHOUT REALLY
WANTING TO...

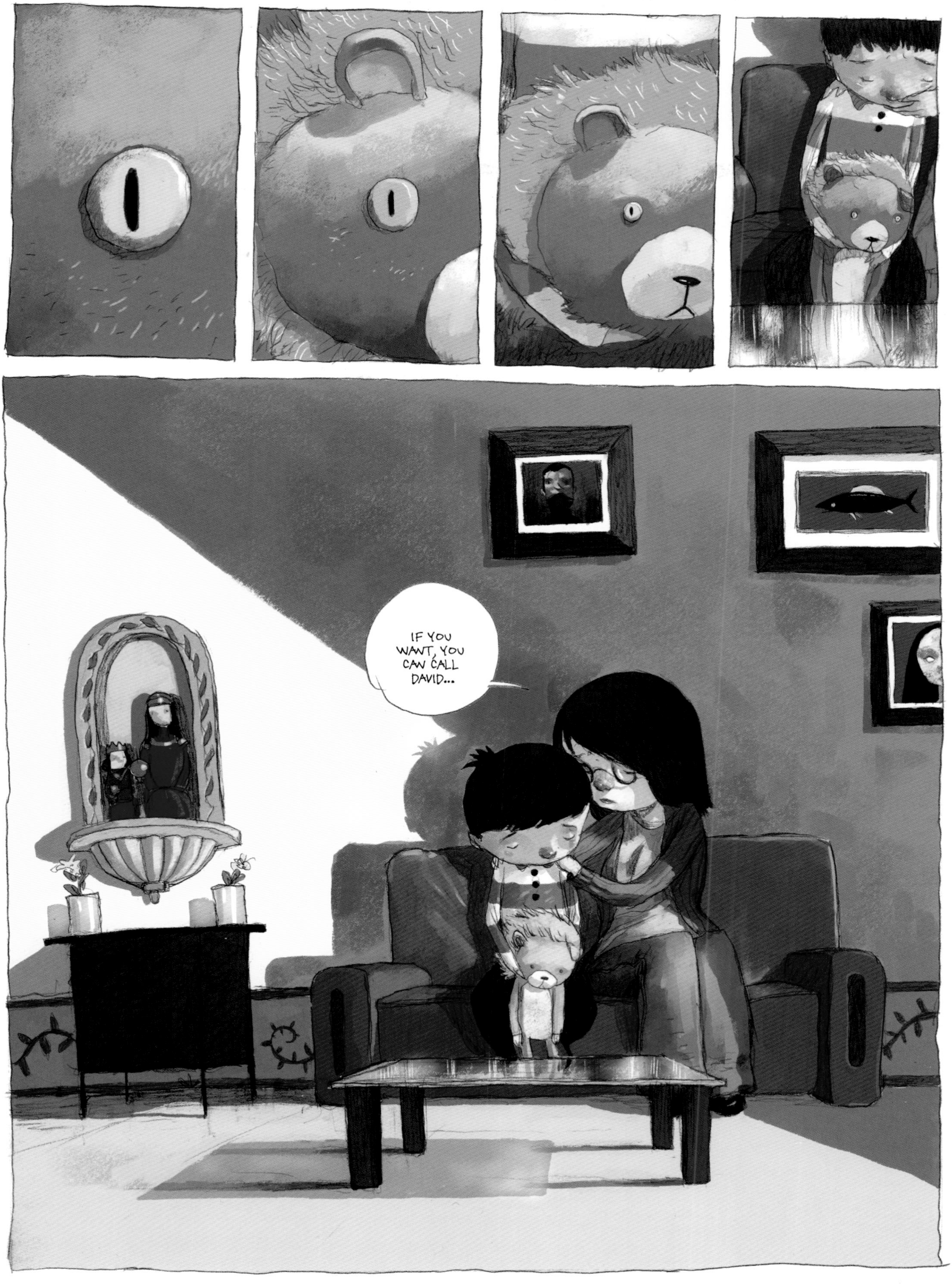
IF YOU WANT, YOU CAN CALL DAVID...

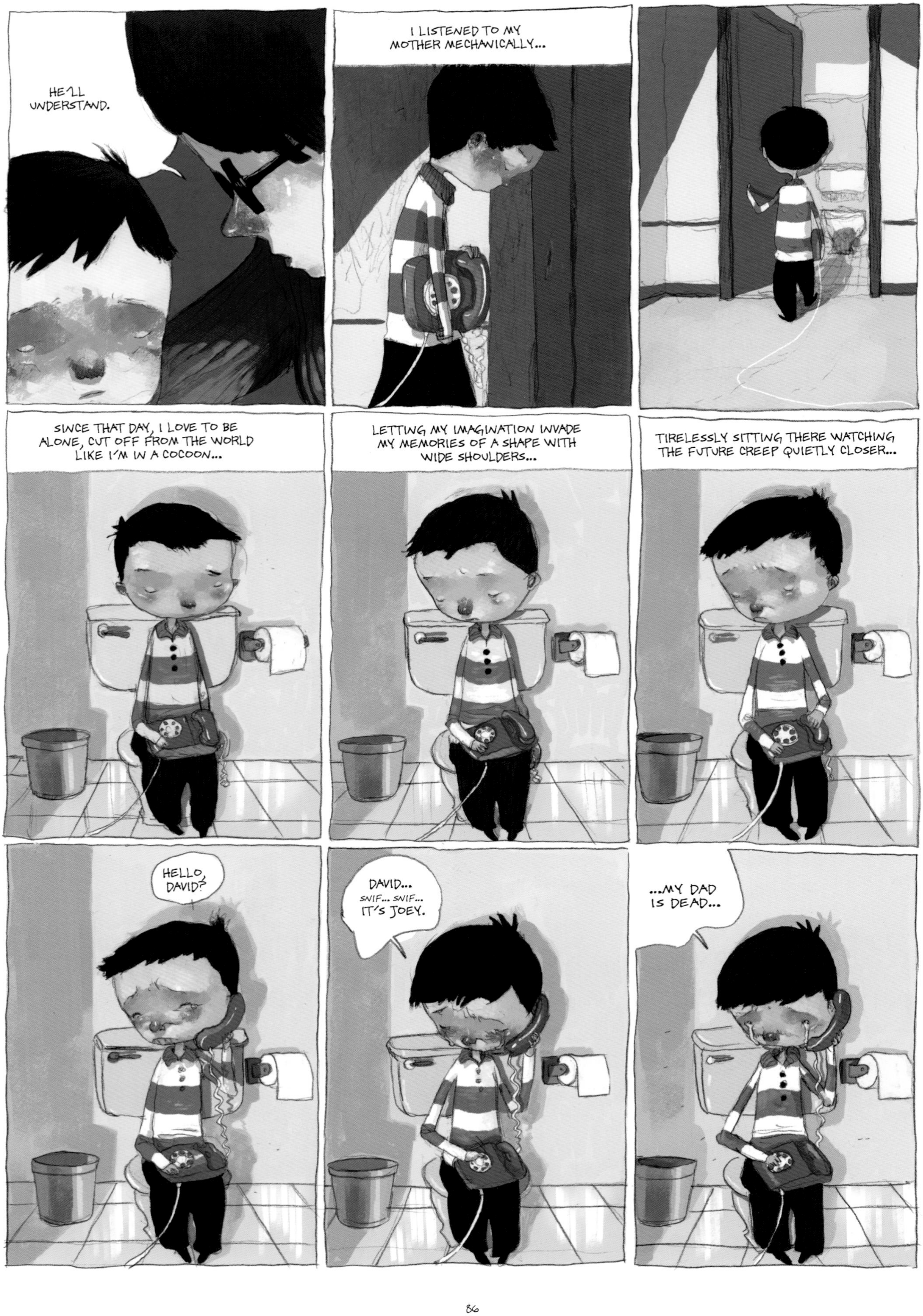
HE'LL UNDERSTAND.
I LISTENED TO MY MOTHER MECHANICALLY...
SINCE THAT DAY, I LOVE TO BE ALONE, CUT OFF FROM THE WORLD LIKE I'M IN A COCOON...
LETTING MY IMAGINATION INVADE MY MEMORIES OF A SHAPE WITH WIDE SHOULDERS...
TIRELESSLY SITTING THERE WATCHING THE FUTURE CREEP QUIETLY CLOSER...
HELLO, DAVID?
DAVID... SNIF... SNIF... IT'S JOEY.
...MY DAD IS DEAD...

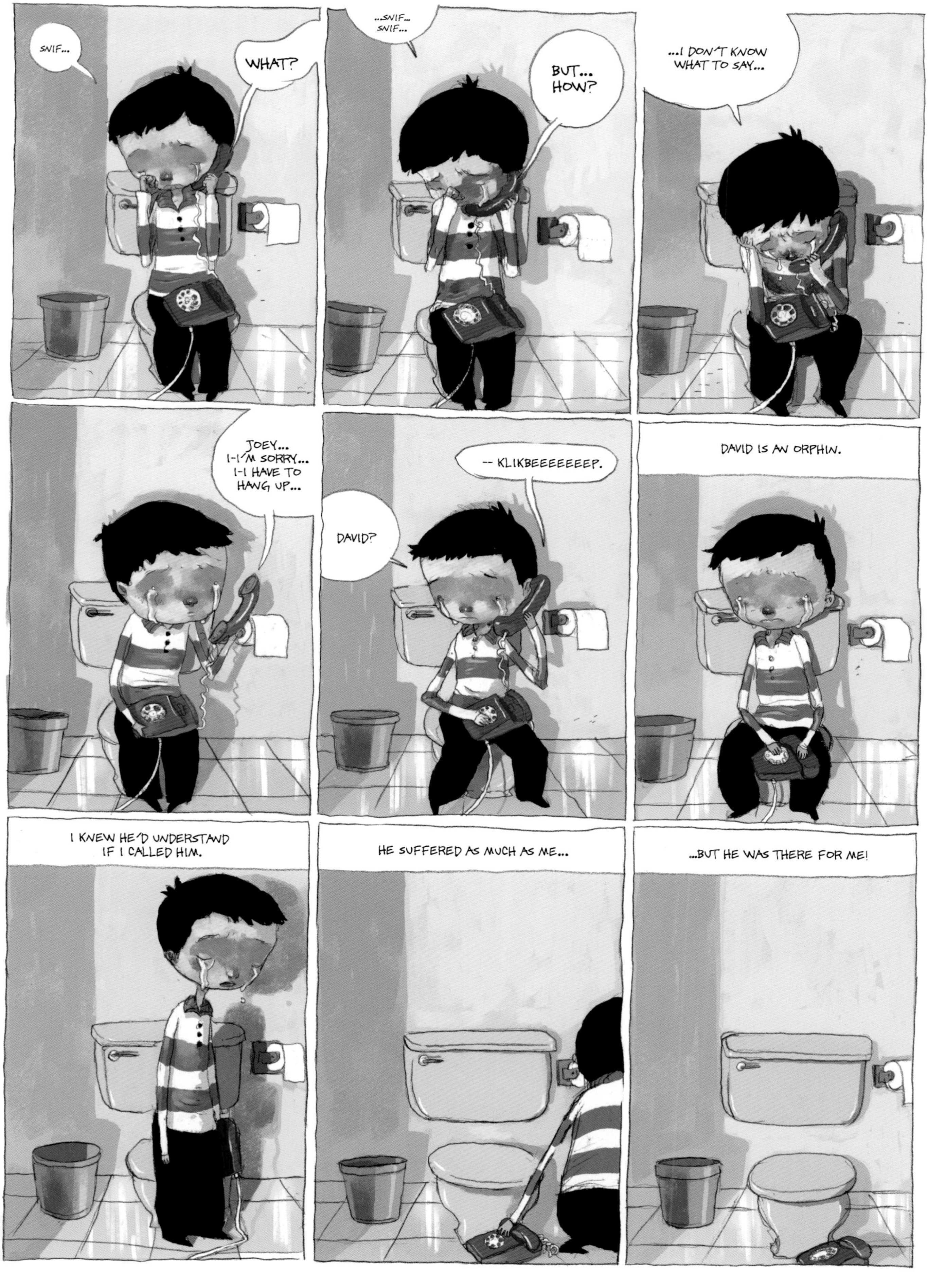
SNIF...
WHAT?
...SNIF... SNIF...
BUT... HOW?
...I DON'T KNOW WHAT TO SAY...
JOEY... I-I'M SORRY... I-I HAVE TO HANG UP...
DAVID?
-- KLIKBEEEEEEEP.
DAVID IS AN ORPHIN.
I KNEW HE'D UNDERSTAND IF I CALLED HIM.
HE SUFFERED AS MUCH AS ME...
...BUT HE WAS THERE FOR ME!

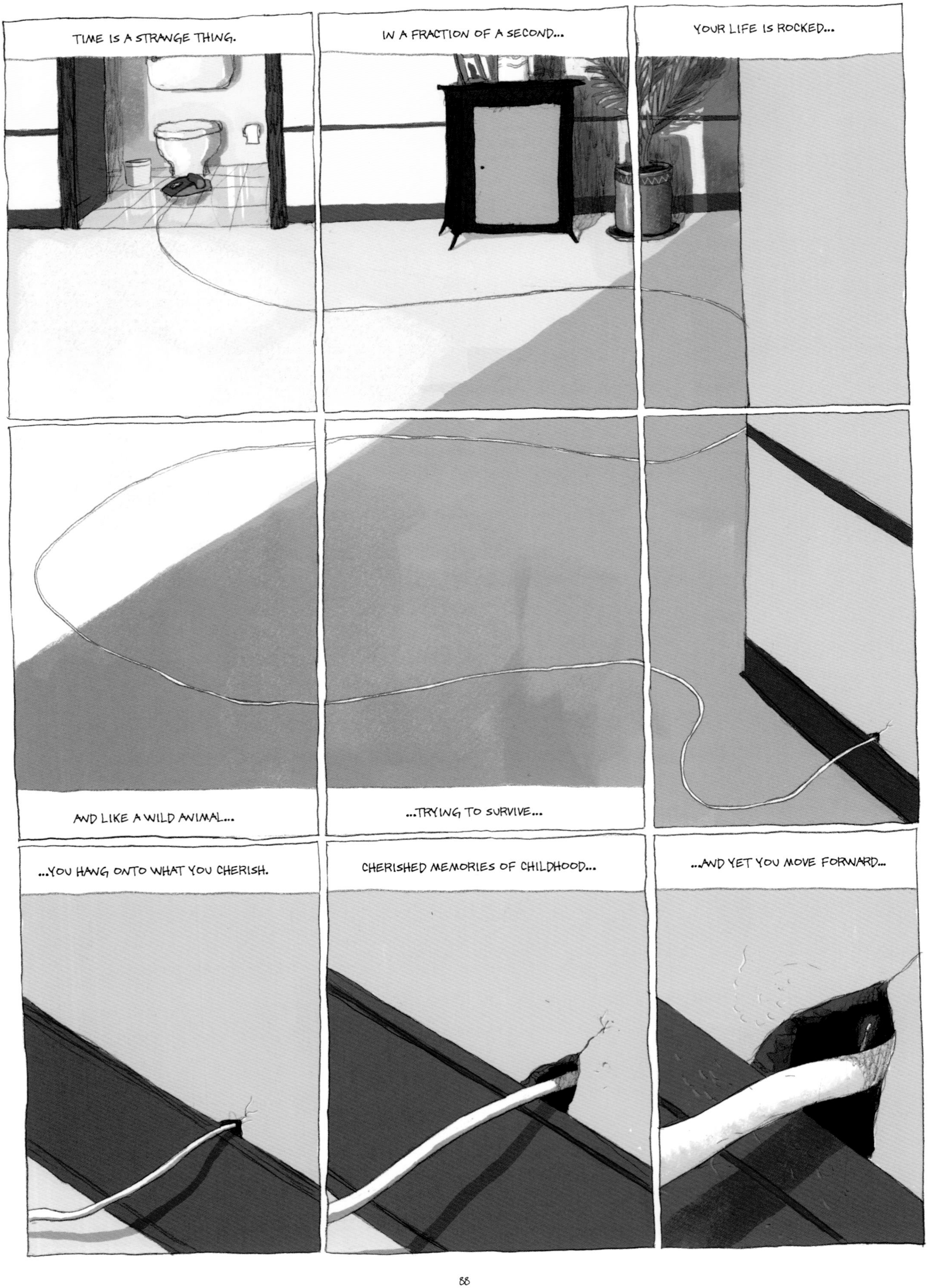
TIME IS A STRANGE THING.
IN A FRACTION OF A SECOND...
YOUR LIFE IS ROCKED...
AND LIKE A WILD ANIMAL...
...TRYING TO SURVIVE...
...YOU HANG ONTO WHAT YOU CHERISH.
CHERISHED MEMORIES OF CHILDHOOD...
...AND YET YOU MOVE FORWARD...

...AS AN ADULT!

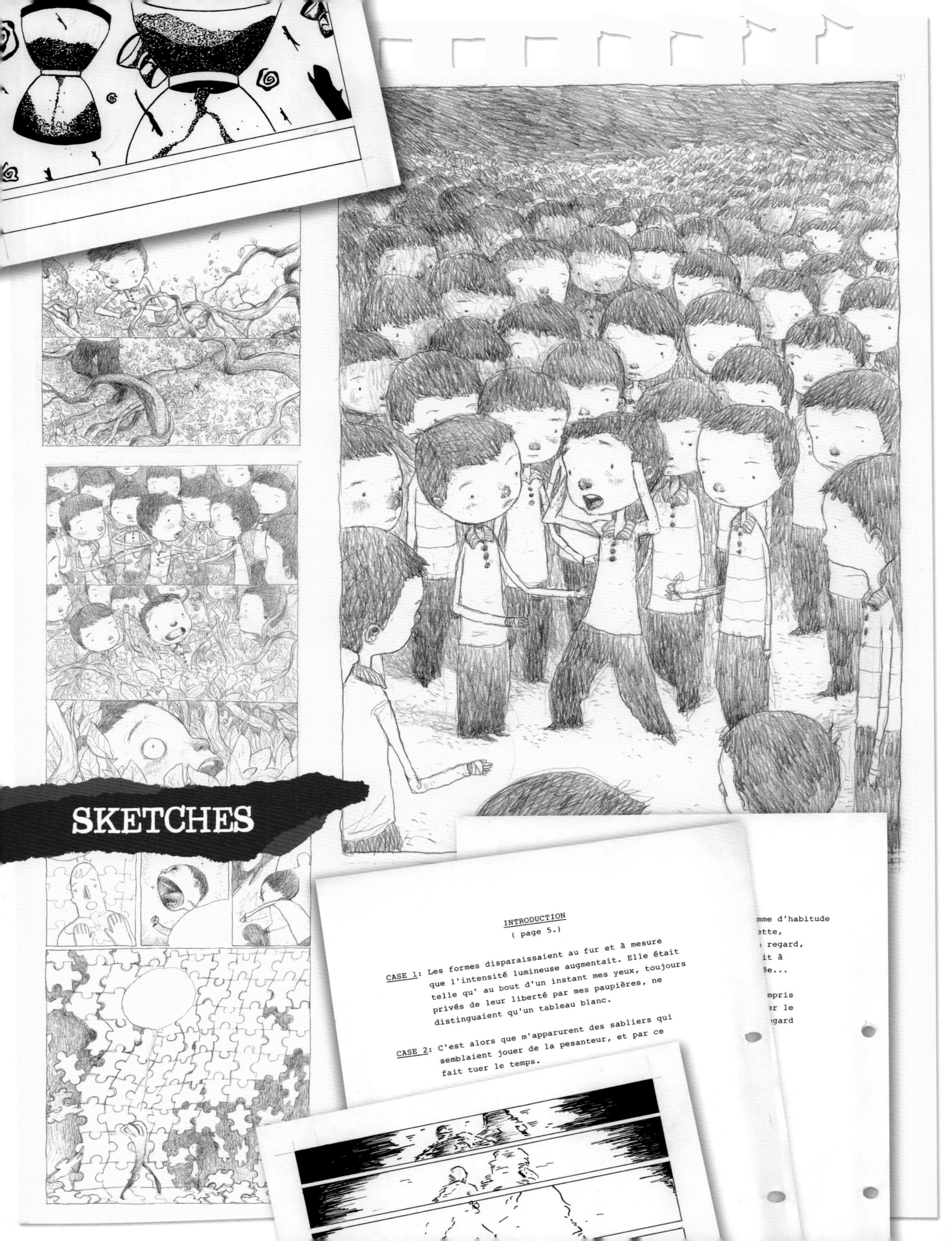
SKETCHES
INTRODUCTION
( page 5.)
CASE 1: Les formes disparaissaient au fur et à mesure que l'intensité lumineuse augmentait. Elle était telle qu' au bout d'un instant mes yeux, toujours privés de leur liberté par mes paupières, ne distinguaient qu'un tableau blanc.
CASE 2: C'est alors que m'apparurent des sabliers qui semblaient jouer de la pesanteur, et par ce fait tuer le temps.
mme d'habitude
ette,
regard,
it à
ée...
mpris
er le
egard

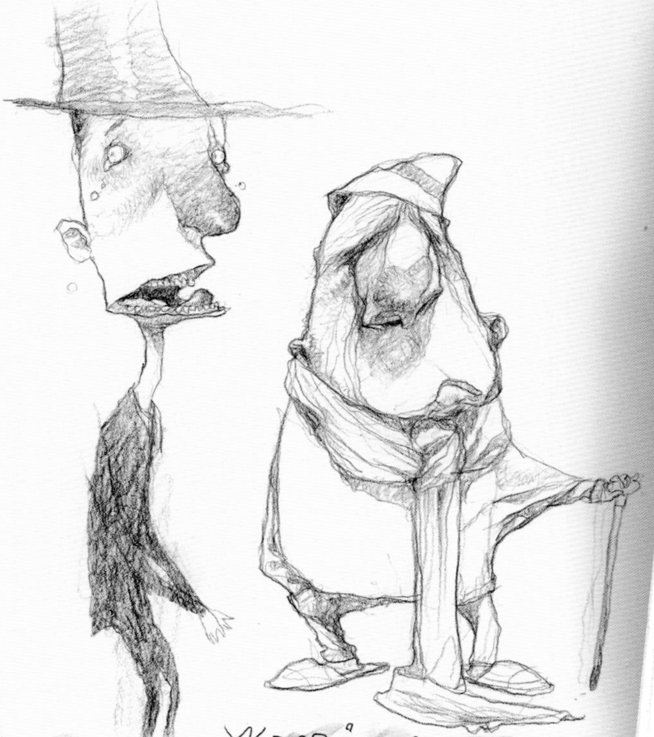

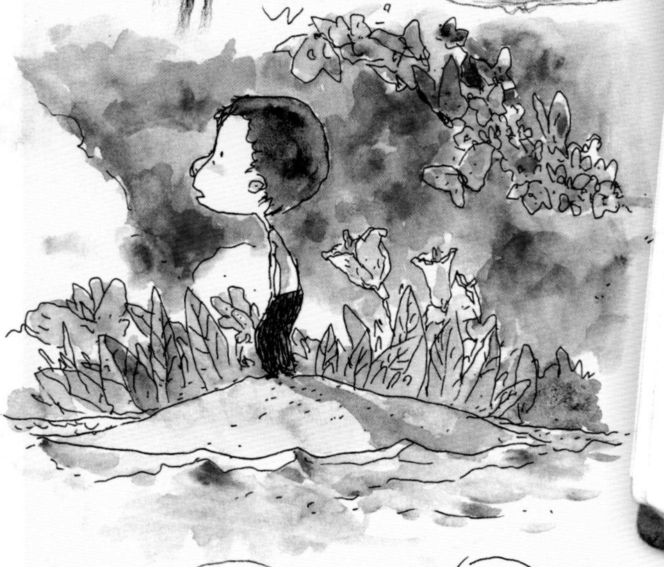

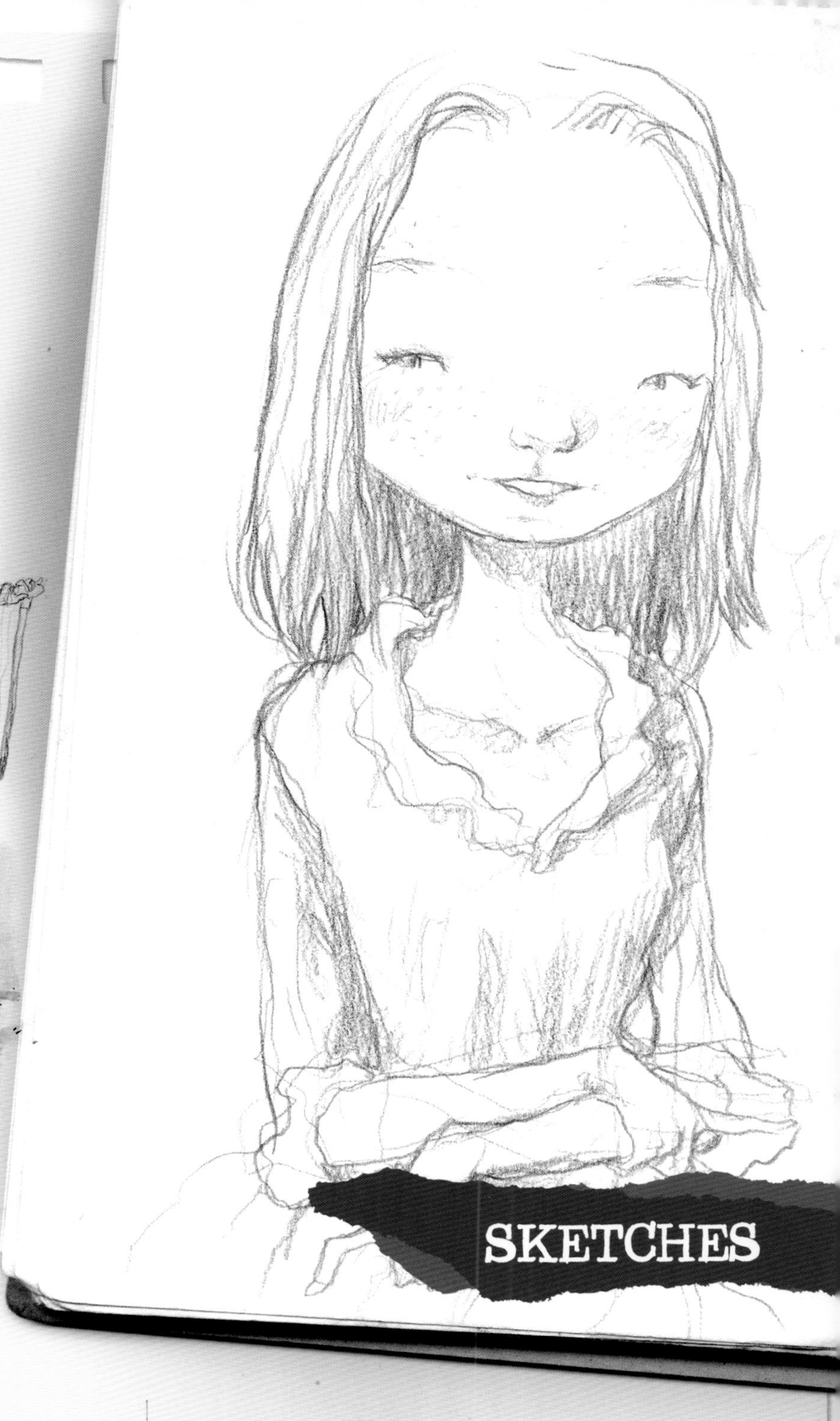

# SKETCHES

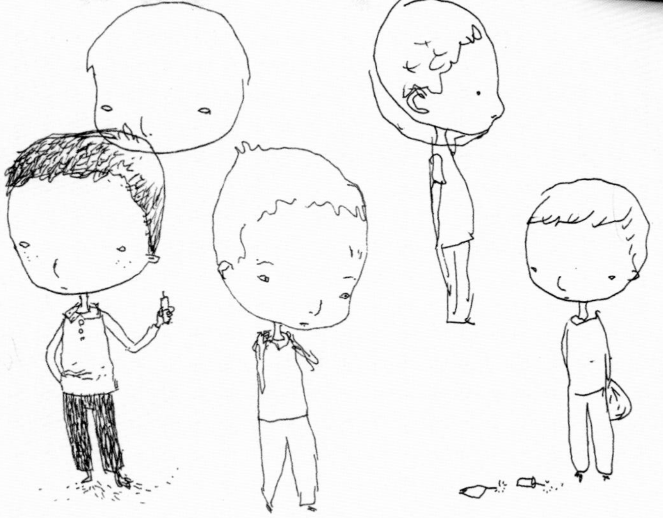

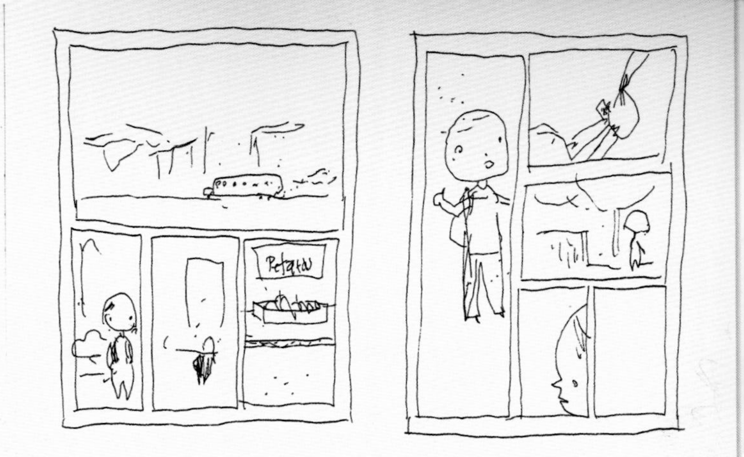

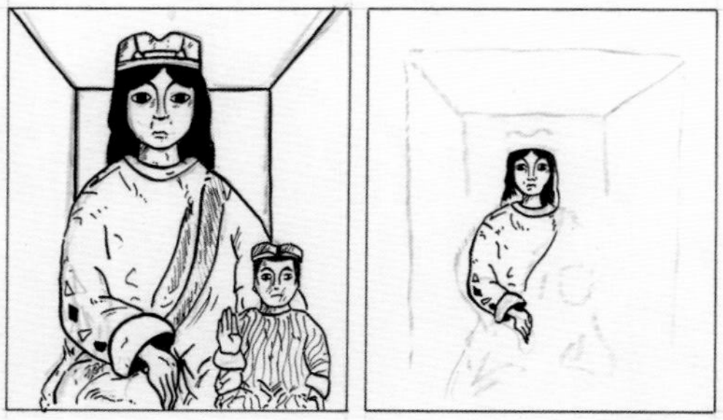

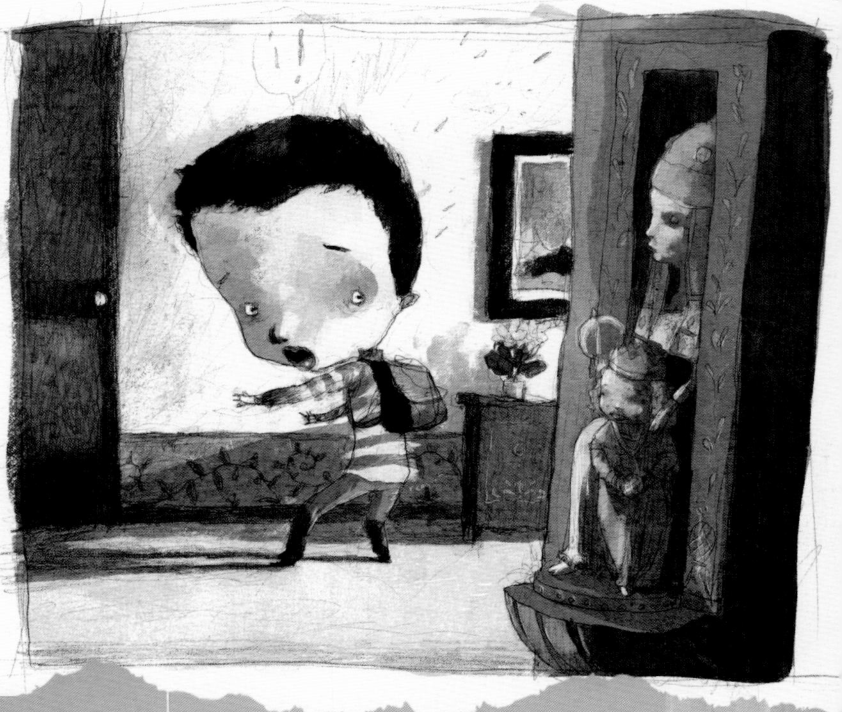

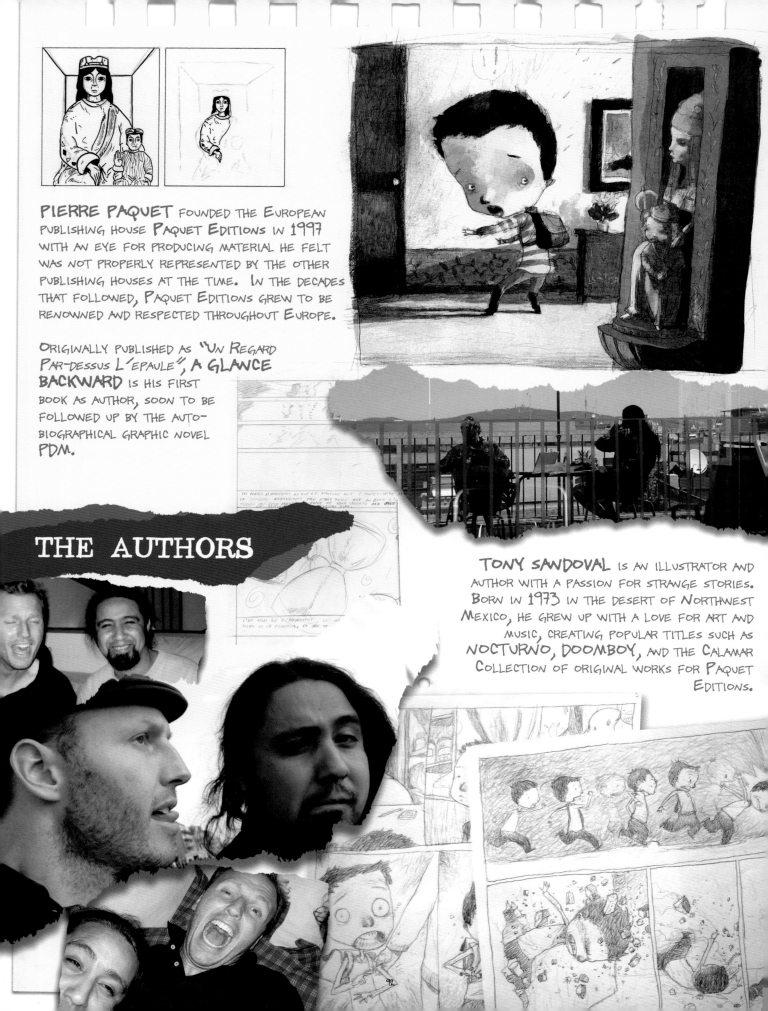

**PIERRE PAQUET** founded the European publishing house Paquet Editions in 1997 with an eye for producing material he felt was not properly represented by the other publishing houses at the time. In the decades that followed, Paquet Editions grew to be renowned and respected throughout Europe.

Originally published as "Un Regard Par-dessus L'epaule", **A GLANCE BACKWARD** is his first book as author, soon to be followed up by the auto-biographical graphic novel **PDM**.

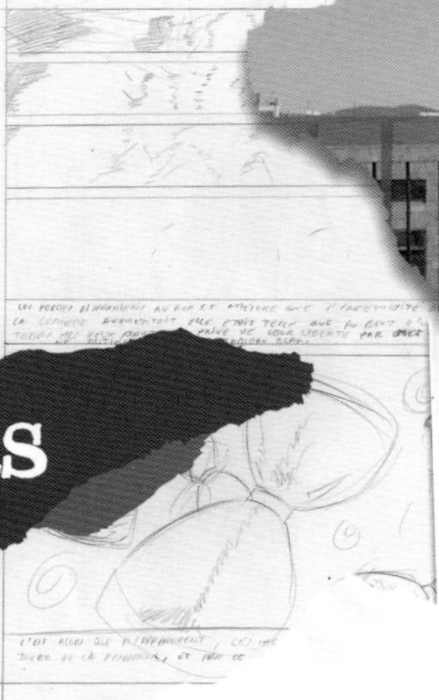

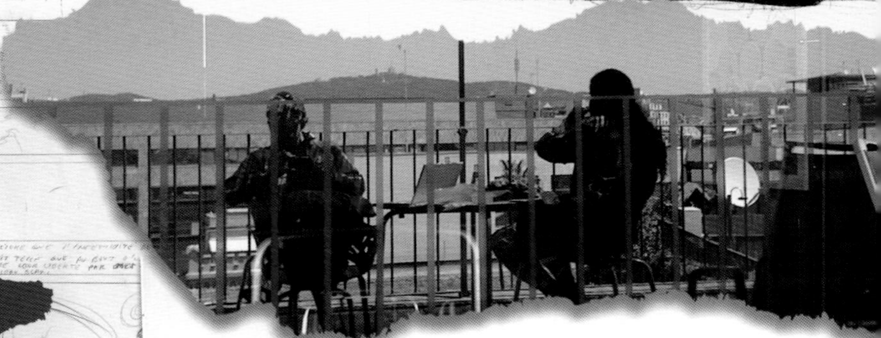

# THE AUTHORS

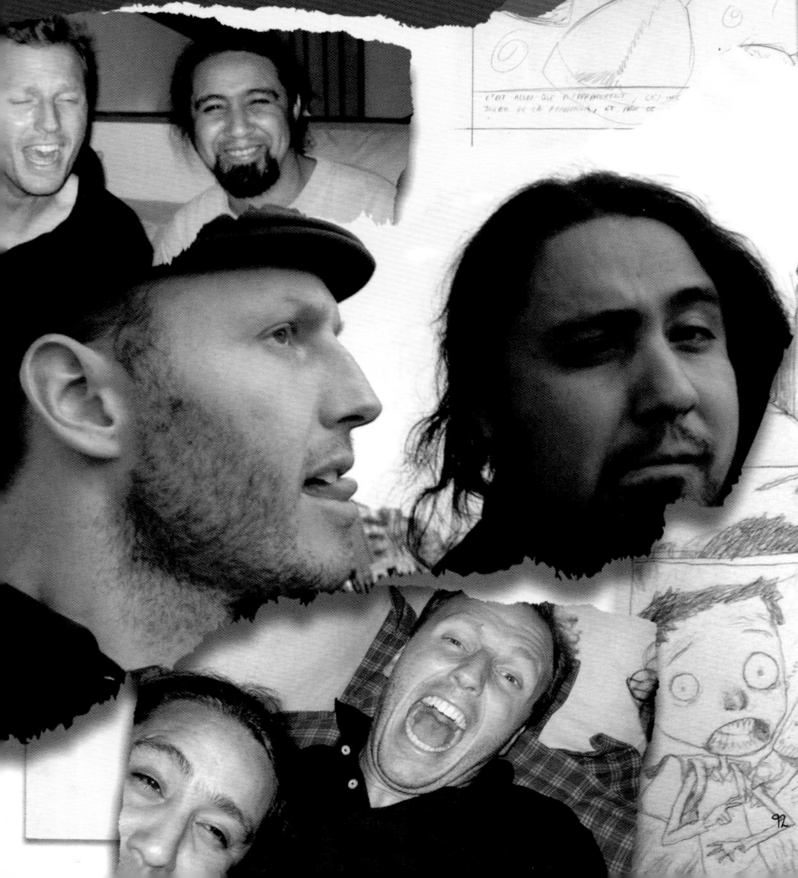

**TONY SANDOVAL** is an illustrator and author with a passion for strange stories. Born in 1973 in the desert of Northwest Mexico, he grew up with a love for art and music, creating popular titles such as **NOCTURNO**, **DOOMBOY**, and the Calamar Collection of original works for Paquet Editions.

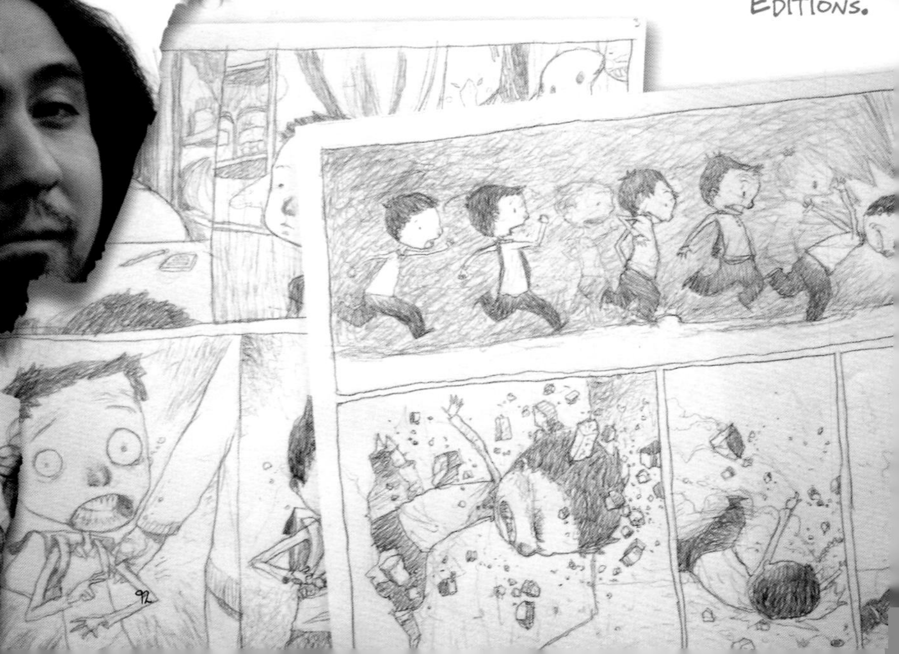

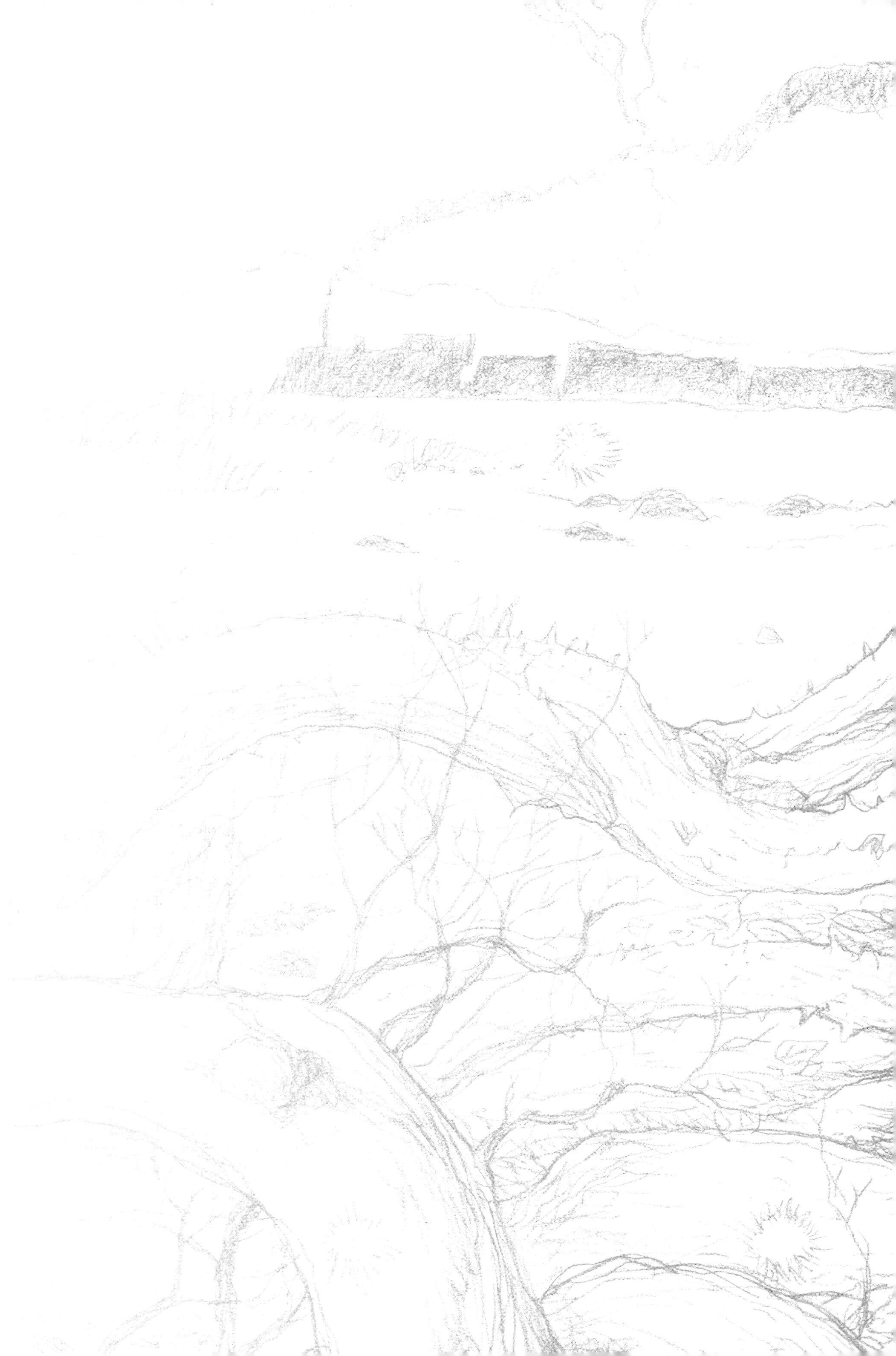